# THE

# KID'S
# GUIDE TO
# CHICAGO

1st
edition

## Eileen Ogintz

# gpp®
travel

Guilford, Connecticut

Thank you to Meghan McCloskey and Jonathan Boydston for their research
help and to Melissa Miller, a teacher and graduate education student in
Chicago, for contributing the games and interviewing local kids. Also thank
you to the campers from Camp Nebagamon in Wisconsin and Camp Kamaji
in Minnesota who live in Chicago and offered their tips to visiting kids.

All the information in this guidebook is subject to change.
We recommend that you call ahead to obtain current
information before traveling.

To buy books in quantity for corporate use
or incentives, call **(800) 962-0973**
or e-mail **premiums@GlobePequot.com.**

Editor: Amy Lyons
Project Editor: Lauren Brancato
Layout: Maggie Peterson
Text Design: Sheryl Kober

Illustrations licensed by Shutterstock.com

ISBN 978-0-7627-9231-3

Printed in the United States of America
10 9 8 7 6 5 4 3 2 1

# Contents

1   Welcome to the Windy City   1

2   Exploring Chicago's Many Neighborhoods   15

3   Ferris Wheels, Water Taxis & a Museum Just for Kids   29

4   Outer Space, Dinosaurs, Stingrays & Sharks   41

5   Paintings, Armor, Tiny Houses & Free Concerts   57

6   Lions, Gorillas, Polar Bears & the Beach   73

7   Deep-Dish Pizza, Flaming Cheese, Hot Dogs & Souvenirs   89

8   Music & Theater   105

9   Play Ball!   117

10   Beyond Chicago: Sand Dunes, Waterslides & Bears   129

What a Trip!   143

Index   148

# 1

# Welcome to the Windy City

# It was a windy Sunday in fall that changed Chicago forever.

Travel back in time to October 8, 1871, when Chicago was a city of wooden buildings. A fire started in a barn owned by Patrick and Catherine O'Leary on the southwest side of the city.

Legend has it that a cow kicked over a lantern, but historians are not convinced that is how the fire started. Some believe that Daniel "Peg Leg" Sullivan who lived across the street accidentally started the fire when he was in the barn that night; others believe a meteor shower started a fire in the hay in the barn.

Whatever the reason, the fire spread quickly because the summer had been so dry, burning an area 4 miles long and nearly a mile wide, destroying more than 17,000 buildings, and leaving nearly 100,000 people homeless.

## DID YOU KNOW?

Chicago has more than 36 annual parades.

The Chicago River is dyed green for St. Patrick's Day.

No matter how cold it is, 1,500 people jump into Lake Michigan the first Sunday in March (chicagopolarplunge.org).

The central business district burned to the ground. So did City Hall and miles of road and sidewalks. **The Chicago Water Tower** (806 N. Michigan Ave.) was one of just five public buildings that survived. You can still see it today. You can also see where the fire started, which is now the **Chicago Fire Academy** (558 W. De Koven St.; 312-747-7238).

As you look around the great city of Chicago and its amazing skyline, think about that fire and the strength of Chicagoans. If not for that terrible fire, Chicago wouldn't be the beautiful city it is today, famous for its skyscrapers—including the world's first, which was built after the fire—and one of the country's best firefighting forces. Some had said at the

A LOCAL KID SAYS:
"Chicago is one of the world's greatest cities!"
—Ella, 15

time that the horse-drawn firefighting equipment was no match for the flames.

Famous architects came from around the world to help rebuild—this time using other construction materials rather than wood—and donations flooded in. By 1893, the World Expo could showcase the "new" Chicago, complete with the world's first Ferris wheel and a new gum called Juicy Fruit made by the Wrigley Company. The **Museum of Science and Industry** (5700 Lake Shore Dr.; 773-684-1414; msichicago.org) grew out of what had been the Expo's fine arts building.

Today, of course, Chicago is a big city that's home to lots of parents, kids, and many immigrants from around the world. Listen to the languages people are speaking—everything from Arabic to Spanish to Chinese.

There's **Chicago's famous lakefront** where you can ride bikes or go to the beach in the summer. Some of the best kid-friendly museums in the country are here, along with parks and playgrounds and the chance to see professional sports no matter what the season.

Maybe you want to start in the "Loop" (Chicago talk for downtown) where you'll find some of Chicago's most beautiful and famous buildings, including the **Willis Tower** (233 S. Wacker Dr.; 312-875-9447; theskydeck.com). Your parents probably remember that Willis Tower used to be called Sears Tower.

{ **What's Cool?** A boat tour on the Chicago River—the only river in the world that flows backward. This was a huge public works project completed in the early 1890s that saved Chicago from waterborne diseases.

The **John Hancock Observatory** offers lots of fun for kids (875 N. Michigan Ave.; 312-751-3681; jhochicago .com); there's even a Kid's Zone on the website. Here you will learn all about John Hancock, ride in fast elevators, and meet Seemore Miles, the official mascot of the observatory. In the winter you can ice-skate at 1,000 feet above sea level at **Skating in the Sky** (Jan to Apr 9am to 11pm).

Take a stroll. It's easy to get around because the Loop is laid out like a grid. Check out the amazing Jean Dubuffet sculpture, ***Monument with Standing Beast*** (100 W. Randolph St.; cityofchicago .org) outside the James R. Thompson Center, which

A LOCAL KID SAYS:
"Don't go home without a picture of yourself on the ledge of the Willis Tower."
—Allison, 12

{ **What's Cool?** Riding the "L" through the Loop. The L is the nickname of Chicago's public transit system, and the Loop is what Chicago's downtown is called because the area is encircled by the elevated train tracks.

might be the oddest-shaped building you've seen in a big city. The **Richard J. Daley Center** (50 W. Washington St., Daley Plaza; thedaleycenter.com) is most famous for the huge sculpture by Picasso. In summer, there are concerts and a farmers' market outside on Thursday; in winter, the city's official Christmas tree stands here along with a big traditional German holiday market.

Don't miss the **Chicago Cultural Center** (78 E. Washington St.; 312-744-6630; chicago culturalcenter.org), where you'll find the Chicago Office of Tourism visitor information center and the world's largest Tiffany glass dome.

# A City of Firsts

Chicago may be called the Second City—coming in after New York—but it sure is a city of firsts and introduced to us a lot of things we take for granted today:

- Roller skates
- Cracker Jacks
- Zippers
- Cafeterias
- Hostess Twinkies
- The All-Star Game of major league baseball
- Spray paint
- Pinball games
- Malted milk shakes
- Ferris wheels

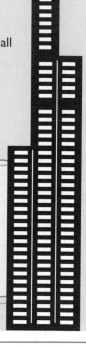

## DID YOU KNOW?

The world's first skyscraper was built in Chicago in 1884. Today Chicago is home to the tallest skyscraper in the Western Hemisphere, the Willis Tower (formerly known as the Sears Tower)—108 stories high.

# Traveling Greener in Chicago

Even before you were born, Chicago has been working to be "green" and has become one of the most environmentally friendly big cities in the country with green roofs, hundreds of parks, and more hotels that have been certified with a Green Seal than any other city in the country. How you can do your part when you visit:

- Use a reusable water bottle. It will become a souvenir when you put stickers on it from all the places you've visited in Chicago.

- Turn off the lights and air conditioner in your hotel room when you leave.

- Recycle.

- Reuse towels in the hotel room.

- Take shorter showers to conserve water.

- Use public transportation when you can.

## DID YOU KNOW?

Chicago has more than 500 "green" roofs where things grow on top of buildings—that's seven million square feet! There's even one on City Hall!

## TELL THE ADULTS:

Touring cities isn't only about famous sites and museums—especially in Chicago. Leave a lot of time to explore the city's neighborhoods, play soccer in the park, go to a baseball or basketball game, or just take a ride around the Loop on the L. You'll find the *real* Chicago in neighborhoods where families like yours live. Most important, get the kids involved in the planning:

- Let them help plan the itinerary starting at the official Chicago tourism website: choosechicago.com.

- *Time Out Chicago Kids* (timeoutchicagokids.com) has a list of current kid-friendly events.

- Take a virtual tour of museums and tourist sites before you visit and decide

### DID YOU KNOW?

Fire Prevention Week started in Chicago on the 40th anniversary of the Great Chicago Fire. Today, this is a national event always commemorated in early October to educate parents and kids about fire safety.

where you want to focus your attention. If you plan to go to many of the city's major museums and attractions, consider getting a **Chicago CityPASS** (citypass.com/Chicago), which will save you significant money on admissions and also allow you to bypass some of the lines.

- If the kids are old enough, encourage each to plan a day of your visit. At the very least, make sure each person in the family has a say in the itinerary.

- Consider a free customized tour for your family with one of the local volunteers from **Chicago Greeter** (chicago greeter.com). They welcome the opportunity to show off their city. The service matches guides based on your interests. Just make sure to register 10 business days in advance.

# CHICAGO WORD SEARCH

Find and circle the hidden words!

| | |
|---|---|
| Big Shoulders | City That Works |
| Ferris Wheel | Hancock |
| Obama | Second City |
| The Loop | Willis Tower |
| Windy City | Wrigley Field |

```
W  R  I  G  L  E  Y  F  I  E  L  D  F
I  U  A  B  V  B  R  P  N  T  B  Z  E
N  M  B  M  R  I  O  A  R  H  P  A  R
D  T  R  R  B  G  E  B  I  E  B  R  R
Y  P  E  C  I  S  A  C  M  L  Y  A  I
C  I  T  Y  T  H  A  T  W  O  R  K  S
I  I  S  Q  L  O  R  I  V  O  H  O  W
T  D  E  Z  A  U  N  O  M  P  E  B  H
Y  N  G  Y  I  L  C  J  A  R  G  A  E
S  E  C  O  N  D  C  I  T  Y  I  M  E
Y  F  E  G  E  E  H  L  R  E  M  A  L
J  U  R  H  D  R  H  A  N  C  O  C  K
E  C  N  A  S  S  R  S  E  W  R  O  N
I  B  E  T  J  L  W  Q  O  P  D  B  C
N  M  W  I  L  L  I  S  T  O  W  E  R
```

*See page 154 for the answers!*

**What's Cool?** Stepping out in a suspended glass box at Skydeck Chicago, more than 1,000 feet in the air at the Willis Tower. On a clear day you can see four states—Illinois, Michigan, Wisconsin, and Indiana.

2

Exploring Chicago's
Many Neighborhoods

# Got your sneakers on?

The best way to see where Chicago kids live and play is to explore the city's neighborhoods. And you'll want your comfiest shoes to walk around in. Leave the car parked too.

It's much easier—and more fun—to get around Chicago by public transportation—buses, trains, and boats. You can take a water taxi—or rent a bike. Chicago has more than 18 miles of bike paths along the lake!

Even if you explore just one or two of Chicago's neighborhoods, you'll see that the city is a lot more than skyscrapers and museums. It's a place where families, many from other parts of the world—Mexico, Poland, China, Greece, Vietnam, and India among them—live, work, go to school, and, of course, play! They have names like Bucktown and

A LOCAL KID SAYS:
"I like to just look around at the buildings downtown."
—Ian, 11

**What's Cool?** Taking a stroll on the Riverwalk along the Chicago River's south side. You can get to it by going down the stairs on any of the river's bridges.

Wicker Park and Logan Square. There's Greektown along Halsted Street and Little Italy along Taylor.

In addition to the **Loop,** which is Chicago's center; **Near North,** where you'll find Navy Pier; and the **South Loop,** where you'll find famous museums, you can visit:

- **The Gold Coast:** So named because its mansions have attracted wealthy families for more than a century. You might want to go to the top of the **John Hancock Center** (875 N. Michigan Ave.; 312-751-3681; jhochicago.com) here for a great view of the city or take a walk on Oak Street Beach.

- **Old Town and Lincoln Park:** The famous Lincoln Park is the city's largest—it stretches for 6 miles (chicago parkdistrict.com)! It has one of the last free zoos in the country and North Avenue Beach, Chicago's most popular stretch of sand. Ready for beach volleyball?

- **Lakeview and Wrigleyville** (1060 W. Addison St.; 773-404-2827; wrigleyville.org) are home to Wrigley Field and Cubs fans, who descend whenever the Cubbies are in town. Take a picture at the entrance to Wrigley Field!

A LOCAL KID SAYS:
"No one can leave Chicago unless they have taken lots of pictures as a souvenir. I think overall that is the best souvenir—better than toys."
—Natalia, 10

- **Uptown:** With Little Saigon and Andersonville, famous for its Swedish shops and eats, you can explore the food of different cultures. Stop in at the **Swedish Bakery** (5348 N. Clark St.; 773-561-8919; swedish bakery.com) or have a dish of Vietnamese noodles. You can also visit **Graceland Cemetery** (4001 N. Clark St.; 773-525-1105; gracelandcemetery.org) where many famous Chicagoans are buried. Check out the grave of National League founder William Hulbert—the tombstone looks like a baseball!

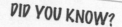

## DID YOU KNOW?

Lake Michigan is Chicago's only eastern border.

Chicago has 40 blocks of underground walkways that people use in the winter. Unfortunately they don't all connect! Look for Pedway signs above ground to find where the entrances are (cityofchicago.org).

Chicago has more than 100 neighborhoods.

■ **Ukrainian Village:** Check out amazing churches. One of them has 13 domes—St. Nicholas Ukrainian Catholic Cathedral (stnicholaschicago.org).

■ **Pilsen** is home to the city's Mexican community. Grab a churro! You'll also find the spot where the Great Chicago Fire began here (between Clinton and Jefferson Streets). And the famous Pilsen murals are all over the buildings here.

■ **Hyde Park:** This is home to the University of Chicago—and President Obama (he lived in an area along Kenwood). These days, you can't really get close to his house on Greenwood Avenue, but you can go to his barber at the **Hyde Park Hair Salon** (5234 S. Blackstone Ave.; 773-493-6028) and check out his glass-encased barber chair. Ready for a trim?

A VISITING KID SAYS:
"Make sure you look out the window on the L! Coming into downtown, you get to see the whole skyline, plus a bunch of other cool buildings."
—Marley, 11, Grand Rapids, MI

{ **What's Cool?** Hunting for "treasures" at the Chicago Antique Market—really a flea market—the last Sunday of the month on Randolph Street (randolphstreetmarket.com).

# Celebrate!

Chicagoans celebrate their culture and holidays all year long.

**JANUARY:** The Chinese New Year Parade (chicagochinatown .org) lights up the winter with colorful floats, dances, and special gift exchanges.

**FEBRUARY:** Black History Month is marked with special events and exhibits across the city.

**MARCH:** The St. Patrick's Day Parade is one the country's largest (chicagostpatsparade.com).

The Greek Independence Day Parade is held in Greektown toward the end of March (greektownchicago.org).

**MAY:** Cinco de Mayo Festival and Parade are held the first Sunday in May (cincodemayochicago.com).

## DID YOU KNOW?

Colonel Robert McCormick, the owner of the *Chicago Tribune*, collected rocks from famous buildings and monuments around the world to use on his Tribune Tower (435 N. Michigan Ave.; 312-222-3994; tribune .com) on Michigan Avenue. You can see more than 120 of them embedded around the tower's base today. A piece from New York's World Trade Center has been added. How many can you count?

A VISITING KID SAYS:
"I always have money in my pocket for souvenirs. In Chicago you can buy toy police cars or models of buildings."
—Vincenzo, 14, Austin, TX

**JULY:** Independence Day Fireworks and "Taste of Chicago," one of the premier outdoor food festivals, both fall in this month (cityofchicago.org).

**OCTOBER:** "Chicagoween" at Daley Plaza comes complete with the Haunted Village (cityofchicago.org).

**NOVEMBER:** The Magnificent Mile Lights Festival kicks off the holidays with the lighting of North Michigan Avenue's million lights (magnificentmilelightsfestival.com). And if you can brave the cold, come out for Chicago's Thanksgiving Day Parade (chicago festivals.org).

**DECEMBER:** Winter Wonder-Fest at Navy Pier (winter wonderfest.com) draws crowds with rides, skating, a huge indoor lights display, and more.

# Staying Safe on Vacation

- Write down the name and phone number of the hotel where you are staying. Also, write down your parents' phone numbers—or put them in your own phone.

- Never approach a vehicle unless you know the owner and are accompanied by an adult.

- Practice "what-if" situations with your parents. What should you do if you get lost in a museum? On a city street? Who should you ask for help?

- Wherever you are, decide on a central, easy-to-locate spot to meet if you get separated.

- Only ask uniformed people for help if you get lost— police offers, firefighters, store security guards or store clerks, or museum staff wearing official badges or identification badges.

# Chicagoans You Should Know

**Louis Sullivan:** This architect is considered the father of modern skyscrapers.

**Daniel Burnham:** This architect and urban designer developed the 1909 plan that preserved Chicago's lakefront.

**Jane Addams:** She was the first American woman to be awarded the Nobel Peace Prize. She founded Hull House, where immigrants came to learn and inspired a national movement.

**Al Capone:** This gangster might have been the most famous Chicagoan in the world before President Barack Obama.

**Michael Jordan:** He ended his career with the Chicago Bulls with the highest per-game scoring average in NBA history.

## DID YOU KNOW?

For 25 years, Oprah Winfrey taped her show at a studio on the Near West Side (110 N. Carpenter St.).

Chicago is a great place to sample ethnic food especially when you venture into neighborhoods away from the tourist sites downtown. Here are some options to try:

- Flaming cheese and shish kebab in Greektown (greektownchicago.org)

- Vietnamese and Thai noodle dishes in Uptown (Argyle Street)

- Tacos, salsas, and fruit-flavored water on 18th Street in Pilsen

- Indian curry on Devon Avenue

- Swedish pancakes on Clark Street in Andersonville (chicagoandersonville.com)

- Barbecued pork buns in Chinatown (chicago chinatown.org)

- Pasta and Italian ices in Little Italy along Taylor Street

A VISITING KID SAYS:
"Chinatown is one of my favorite neighborhoods to visit for all the good food."
—Maeve, 16, Minneapolis, MN

Draw what you saw today!

# 3

# Ferris Wheels, Water Taxis & a Museum Just For Kids

# Wow! Lake Michigan is big.

Really big. Its shoreline stretches for 22,300 miles—four states long. Can you guess which states? (Illinois, Indiana, Michigan, and Wisconsin, in case you are wondering.) Lake Michigan is the third biggest lake in the entire country! Sailors race across Lake Michigan in the famous Race to Mackinac Island boating event every summer. A lot of kids and their parents like to fish on the lake.

**Navy Pier** (600 E. Grand Ave.; 312-595-7437; navypier .com) is a great place to see the lake. It's also a great place for fun and games, whether you ride the giant Ferris wheel, turn cartwheels in the park, check out the flowers

## DID YOU KNOW?

Lake Michigan is one of the five Great Lakes and the only one located entirely within the US. The other four—Lake Superior, Lake Huron, Lake Erie, and Lake Ontario—are shared by the US and Canada.

Chicagoans get their drinking water from Lake Michigan.

A LOCAL KID SAYS:
"Navy Pier is cool because they also have fireworks there. It is awesome on the Fourth of July."
—Daniel, 17

in the gardens, ride the carousel or the new Transporter FX that can take you to the moon, or shop for souvenirs. You'll find everything from handmade soaps to funny refrigerator magnets to souvenir photos of the **Ferris wheel** in one store called **Oh Yes Chicago!** that just sells Chicago-themed souvenirs. You can **Build-A-Bear** (buildabear.com) on Navy Pier, eat some fudge, top your own ice cream or cupcake at the **Candy Sugar Shoppe** (icandysugarshoppe .com), or sample freshly made **Garrett Popcorn** (garrett popcorn.com), a Chicago tradition for 60 years.

**What's Cool?** Watching the fireworks set to music on Navy Pier over Lake Michigan. There are shows every Wednesday night at 9:30 and Saturday at 10:15 all summer and a special family show on New Year's Eve.

There's even a huge **maze** where you have the chance to stomp out the Great Chicago Fire. You can grab a bite at one of the restaurants here or bring a picnic when the weather is nice or even see an IMAX movie.

Check out the **Crystal Gardens**, a 6-story glass building with an indoor botanical garden that stretches for an acre. The ceiling is 50 feet high! There are more than 80 live palm trees and all kinds of dancing fountains as well as twinkling lights inside.

You'll want to leave plenty of time for the **Chicago Children's Museum,** one of the best children's museums in the entire country right here on Navy Pier (700 E. Grand

A LOCAL KID SAYS:
"The Ferris wheel is my favorite thing at Navy Pier. You can see a lot of Chicago from the top, and it's fun. I also like to walk around, get food, and shop. There are a lot of cool stores to shop at."
—Samantha, 13

{ **What's Cool?** The views from the top of the Navy Pier Ferris wheel. It's open even in the winter.

## DID YOU KNOW?

The 150-foot-high Navy Pier Ferris wheel is modeled after the world's first Ferris wheel that was built for Chicago's 1893 World's Columbian Exposition that was held to commemorate the 400th anniversary of Columbus landing in America. The fair's organizers wanted something to rival the Eiffel Tower, which had been built for the Paris World's Fair of 1889. The new attraction was designed by George W. Ferris, a Pennsylvania bridge builder, and at the time the Ferris wheel was considered an engineering marvel.

Ave.; 312-527-1000; chicagochildrensmuseum.org). There are special play spaces and exhibits for the littlest visitors as well as older kids, and parents will have as much fun exploring and creating as you will.

The hardest part is deciding where to start: Take the **Pegboard Challenge in the Tinkering Lab** and put gears, balls, and other parts together to make your own cause-and-effect reaction—and invention. Design and build your own skyscraper with real tools. Explore the re-creation of a real expedition where a Chicago paleontologist discovered a new type of dinosaur. Create art in a special studio staffed by visiting artists whether you want to paint, print, sketch, or sculpt. Navigate your own boat through locks and dams as you control the water with pulleys, wheels, and pipes. Check out the nearly 100 collections of tiny objects in **Michael's Museum** (inside the Chicago Children's Museum)—everything from toys to dollhouse furniture to jewelry.

Chicago is a great place to start a new collection—or contribute to one you already have. What do you collect?

# Ready to Roll?

There are 18 miles of bike paths along Chicago's lakefront, and Navy Pier is right in the middle. You can rent a bike here or take a tour with a company like **Bike and Roll Chicago** (bikechicago.com). Don't forget a bike helmet! If you go north, you'll be heading toward Lincoln Park. Watch out for the runners! If you go south, you'll go past downtown. If it's summer, you'll see lots of boats in the lake, past Millennium Park and Grant Park. (Don't miss the water show—it happens every 20 minutes from spring through fall.) You might make it to Museum Campus, less than a mile away and home to the Field Museum, the Adler Planetarium, and the Shedd Aquarium. Just make sure to lock up your bike when you stop.

# Play It Safe

Got the firefighter boots on? At the **Chicago Children's Museum** (700 E. Grand Ave.; 312-527-1000; chicagochildrens museum.org) you can put on a firefighter's gear, dispatch fire trucks, slide down a pole, and "drive" the fire truck. The exhibit was developed with the Chicago Fire Department. You'll also learn important fire safety lessons like those offered by the National Fire Protection Association (the website sparky.org offers more games about Sparky the Fire Dog).

When you enter a public building, including a hotel:

- Plan a meeting place with your family in case you get separated in an emergency.

- Locate the exits so you know where to go in case of an emergency.

- React immediately if an alarm sounds or you see smoke. Get out of the building in an orderly fashion.

- Once you have gotten out, stay out. Leave the firefighting to the firefighters!

## TELL THE ADULTS:

Kids might think they are ready for a big attraction—like a 150-foot-high Ferris wheel—only to get there and be frightened. Also some rides, like the giant swing at Navy Pier, can be a tough bet for kids prone to motion sickness.

Scary ride advice:

- They don't have to ride any attraction they don't feel comfortable with, no matter what an older sibling says.

- The ride will be there next time you visit.

- You were scared of something too when you were their age.

- There's always an alternate fun activity.

### DID YOU KNOW?

Adults aren't permitted to enter the Chicago Children's Museum without a child.

A VISITING KID SAYS:
"The rides on the pier are fun, especially the swings. That is my favorite thing I have done in Chicago."
—Luke, 12, Florida

# SECRET WORD PUZZLE

Using the key at the bottom, write the letters under the symbols to figure out the secret phrase.

For example:  = b i r d

\_ \_ \_ \_   \_ \_ \_ \_   \_ \_ \_ \_ \_ \_

\_ \_ \_ \_ \_

a = ✔   b = 🚲   c = 🏙   d = ✈   e = 🎁

f = 🏭   g = 🏛   h = 🏠   i = (road)   j = 🏡

k = 🐝   l = ?   m = !   n = 👁   o = (ship)

p = (path)   q = 🌲   r = (bridge)   s = ✦   t = (boat)

u = 📢   v = (box)   w = ⚑   x = ◀   y = ❤

z = 💐   . = ◼   ! = 🚌   , = (chili)

*See page 154 for the answer.*

Now try and make your own secret messages in the space below.

# 4
# Outer Space, Dinosaurs, Stingrays & Sharks

# Name the place in Chicago

where you can journey into space, travel back in time to when dinosaurs ruled the earth, and get up close with stingrays and belugas.

Stumped?

Welcome to Chicago's huge **Museum Campus,** home to the world-famous Field Museum, the Shedd Aquarium, and the Adler Planetarium—all in one big park.

Where do you want to start?

If you love dinosaurs, you'll want to go to the **Field Museum** (1400 S. Lake Shore Dr.; 312-922-9410; fieldmuseum.org) where you'll not only meet

Sue, the world's most complete *Tyrannosaurus rex* ever found, but you can watch paleontologists clean bones and see every major group of dinosaurs. Of course, there's a lot more at this massive museum than just dinosaur bones! You can:

- Journey through four billion years of life on earth in the Evolving Planet exhibit.

- Shrink to the size of the bug—1/100th of your size— and explore the world from a bug's perspective complete with worm tunnels.

- Travel with museum scientists to remote corners of the world as they work to protect the wilderness and the environment in the Abbott Hall of Conservation Restoring Earth exhibit.

What's Cool? Taking a picture with Sue, the 13-foot-tall *T. rex* at the Field Museum. Check out her 58 teeth!

- Watch a movie that will bring some of the museum's exhibit topics to life in Chicago's only completely digital 3-D theater.

- Explore an ancient Egyptian tomb. It's 5,000 years old. You can see one of the biggest collections of mummies in any US museum and even see how people were mummified in ancient times. Check out the ancient marketplace. How does it compare to a mall?

- When you visit, be sure to check out the museum's temporary exhibits. See if there are any special kids' activities going on.

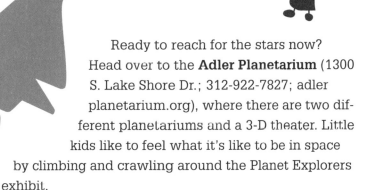

Ready to reach for the stars now? Head over to the **Adler Planetarium** (1300 S. Lake Shore Dr.; 312-922-7827; adler planetarium.org), where there are two different planetariums and a 3-D theater. Little kids like to feel what it's like to be in space by climbing and crawling around the Planet Explorers exhibit.

Everyone loves seeing the *Gemini 12*, the spacecraft flown by astronauts Jim Lovell and Buzz Aldrin. Put on your 3-D glasses and leave the earth behind at one of the Adler's shows. Are you ready to travel a billion light years away?

You can also:

- Take a walk through our solar system and even make your own crater with the Adler's Crater Maker at the Solar System exhibit.

- Get the latest space news in the Cyberspace Gallery.

- Visit a medieval classroom to see how different school was and learn how to use early astronomy tools like sundials in the Astronomy & Culture exhibit.

There was really a time in history when people thought the earth was the center of the universe!

Now it's time to explore the deep—at the **John G. Shedd Aquarium** (1200 S. Lake Shore Dr.; 312-939-2438; sheddaquarium.org). What's your favorite sea creature?

- Watch out for piranhas, spiders, and rays in river channels as you journey in the Amazon.

A VISITING KID SAYS:
"I like the aquarium for the dolphins, penguins, jellyfish, and sharks. I really love watching the dolphin shows so I can see the tricks."
—Veda, 11, Anoka, MN

{ **What's Cool?** Watching the funny penguins at the Shedd Aquarium. Some are only 15 inches tall!

- Watch dolphins jump and belugas dance at Shedd's aquatic show.

- Follow a green sea turtle and get up close to parrotfish and sharks at the Caribbean Reef.

- Laugh at the sea otters and sea lions and listen to the beluga whales "talk" at the Abbott Oceanarium.

- Try on a penguin suit in the Polar Play Zone.

- Watch the divers feed the fish— and tell you about them— in the Caribbean Reef.

Having fun yet? Who knew science could be so entertaining!

# Coal Mines, Miniature Trains & Submarines

Wow! **The Museum of Science and Industry** (5700 S. Lake Shore Dr.; 773-684-1414; msichicago.org) has more than 2,000 exhibits, and new ones are being added all the time. Look around for Science Minors—high school kids who work at the museum and can help you interpret the exhibits.

There's a Fab Lab where you can make almost anything you can think of using software and equipment, watch scientists conduct chemical experiments, creating fire, explosions and sparks, and even become a nature investigator and dig into an owl pellet. (What did that owl eat for lunch?) Check the times when these experiences are offered.

Whatever time of year you come, there are not-to-be-missed exhibits:

A VISITING KID SAYS:
"The Museum of Science and Industry was huge and there were a lot of things to do. My favorite was the tour of the German submarine that was used during WWII."
—Vincenzo, 14, Austin, TX

- Chicago kids always come here at the holidays to see Christmas Around the World and Holidays of Light—there are more than 50 trees decorated by volunteers from Chicago's ethnic communities to show off their holiday traditions.

- Descend into a simulated coal mine and learn what it takes to dig coal out of the ground.

- Explore a U-505 German submarine. Boy the quarters were cramped! This one was captured during World War II.

- Watch a science movie on a giant screen.

- See the Fairy Castle dollhouse that has tiny murals and paintings by Walt Disney, chandeliers with real diamonds and pearls, the tiniest Bible ever written, and statues more than 2,000 years old. It was the "dream" house of a movie star in the 1930s.

**What did you like best?**

# Protecting the Great Lakes

More than 32 million people in the US and Canada rely on the Great Lakes for their drinking water. We depend on the eco-systems the lakes support. But nonnative animals and plants are overtaking the region. More than 180 fish, plants, and other organisms have settled in the Great Lakes Basin and can harm native species by altering their habitats. The Shedd Aquarium conducts research with other Great Lakes organizations to help conserve water and protect native habitats. Volunteers with the Shedd's Great Lakes Program have cleared more than 1,000 pounds of debris through the Adopt-a-Beach program.

## DID YOU KNOW?

The Great Lakes are a one-time gift from glaciers that melted tens of thousands of years ago.

**You can help too:**

- Don't litter, and pick up trash along the lakefront.

- Choose sustainable fish to eat. That means fish that are bountiful. Many populations of fish we like to eat are overfished, and fish farming only adds to the problem. The Shedd Aquarium has created the Rite Bite card that you can download so you will know what seafood is environmentally friendly (sheddaquarium.org). Tilapia is a good choice; farmed salmon isn't.

- Donate unwanted aquatic pets to a school instead of releasing them into a waterway.

- Leave rocks, plants, and other natural objects as you find them.

- Don't feed birds or other wildlife.

# A Dinosaur Named Sue

A flat tire was responsible for one of the greatest finds of dinosaur fossils.

Paleontologist Sue Hendrickson and her team were getting ready to leave the area in South Dakota where they had been searching for fossils when they discovered a flat tire on their truck. While others went into town to repair it, she set out to explore some cliffs not far away.

Hendrickson saw some bones and then even larger ones above her. Soon her team discovered that most of a *Tyrannosaurus rex* had been preserved in the soil. Amazing! Previous finds were usually missing over half their bones. Even most of Sue's teeth were intact.

The fossil hunters also discovered a lot of other fossils of plants and animals that together help scientists to understand what South Dakota looked like when Sue lived 67 million years ago.

The Field Museum, with the help of big companies like Walt Disney Parks and McDonalds and individual donors, ultimately bought Sue for more than $8 million. She arrived in 1997, and millions of people were able to watch the bones being prepared both at the Field Museum in Chicago and at Animal Kingdom in Orlando.

Virtually all parts of Sue's skeleton are preserved. Sue's bone count totals 224 of the 321 known bones, including almost all her belly ribs.

Today not only can you come snout-to-snout with Sue, but you can also examine her skull—it weighs 600 pounds—and learn how scientific thinking about dinosaurs has changed.

**Who is your favorite dino?**

## TELL THE ADULTS:

Visiting a big museum can be overwhelming and exhausting. You can save precious time if you buy your tickets in advance. Here are some ways the Field Museum makes it easier for families—and you can use these same ideas at other museums:

- Download a Family Adventure Tour or pick one up at an information desk.

- Ask about special kid-friendly programming available on the day you visit.

- Stop by an interpretive station offering hands-on activities. That might be finding out what your name looks like in Egyptian hieroglyphs.

- Sign on for a guided tour of some of the museum's most popular exhibits. Check the website for times.

A LOCAL KID SAYS:
"I like to see the Science Theater Shows at the Museum of Science and Industry."
—Anna, 7

- On some Friday nights there are special family workshops at the Field Museum and the chance to sleep over amid some of the most popular exhibitions.

- Check out the interactive Crown PlayLab at the Field Museum for young children, the Polar Play Zone at the Shedd Aquarium, the Clark Family Lab at the Adler Planetarium, and Hands-on Science at the Museum of Science and Industry.

5

Paintings, Armor,
Tiny Houses
& Free Concerts

# Name the place in Chicago

where you can see some of the most famous paintings in the world, gawk at a maze of miniature rooms with furniture tinier than your fingers, check out ancient suits of armor, and create art yourself. You might even be able to talk to a "lion"—well, a person dressed up like a friendly lion.

And when you've had enough, just take a pedestrian bridge to a really cool park where you can jump in a fountain, have a picnic, ice-skate in the winter, or listen to a free concert in the summer.

Welcome to the **Art Institute of Chicago** (111 S. Michigan Ave.; 312-443-3600; artic.edu) and **Millennium Park** (201 E. Randolph St.; 312-742-2963; cityofchicago.org).

A VISITING KID SAYS:
"Pack your swimsuits to play in the fountain at Millennium Park. I love it when it looks like a person is spitting water on you. Also, take time to play around the Bean—it's fun to make yourself look really skinny and tall in the reflection."
—Morganne, 11, Round Rock, TX

The Art Institute is so big that it has more than 4,000 sculptures and 5,000 paintings from all around the world—some thousands of years old—spread out in four buildings. It's the second largest art museum in the entire country with more than 260,000 different works of art.

Millennium Park also is famous for its artwork—including the massive sculpture *Cloud Gate* that Chicagoans have

What's Cool? Taking a picture of yourself with the skyline reflected in the big Cloud Gate sculpture in Millennium Park. Get underneath and touch it! And while you are in the park, go ahead and splash in the famous Crown Fountain—in summer, of course.

nicknamed **"The Bean,"** the **Lurie Garden** (luriegarden
.org), and the **Pritzker Pavilion** (201 E. Randolph St.; 312-
742-1168) that hosts free concerts on most summer nights.
You can even take a free exercise class in the park on
Saturday (yoga maybe?). In summer, look for the **Family
Fun Tent** on the Park's Chase Promenade North, where
there are free kids activities.

A LOCAL KID SAYS:
"The Bean in Millennium Park is like a
house of mirrors but cooler. My favorite
thing to do at the Bean is to look up into
the center and see everyone else in there.
It's the perfect place to spy on someone."
—Samantha, 13

{ **What's Cool?** Watching the colorful fountain sprays at night in the summer at
Buckingham Fountain. Water shoots 150 feet in the air! And it doesn't cost anything
to watch!

But let's start at the museum. Because it's so big, take a virtual tour before you visit and decide what you'd like to see. Some kids like to buy postcards of famous paintings and have a scavenger hunt looking for them in the museum. Some kids like to imagine themselves inside the painting. What would it have been like to live then?

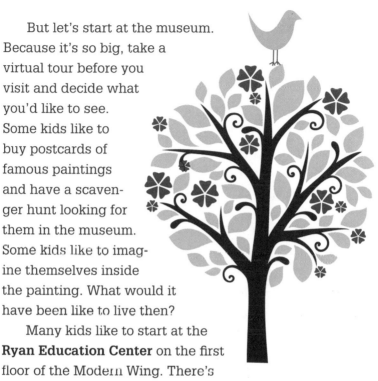

Many kids like to start at the **Ryan Education Center** on the first floor of the Modern Wing. There's a learning center where you can explore the exhibits virtually and find out where you can go in the museum to create your own art.

## DID YOU KNOW?

The three white stripes on the Chicago flag represent the neighborhoods of the North, South, and West sides of the city.

Kids also love the **Thorne Miniature Rooms.** There are 68 of them, and they are tiny models of everything from a Massachusetts room from colonial times to a French castle. They're amazing.

Families also like the **Bluhm Family Terrace** outdoors in the Modern Wing. Check out the sculptures! This is where you'll find the famous pedestrian bridge to Millennium Park.

Check out the **Touch Gallery,** which was designed for those who are visually impaired. Kids like it because it is one place where they are encouraged to touch the art.

Your parents probably want you to see some of the museum's famous paintings, and you will want to see them too. Here are some you may already know:

■ *American Gothic* by Grant Wood of two stern-faced farmers. What do you think they were thinking about to look so downcast?

- *The Old Guitarist* by Pablo Picasso of a poor street guitarist. This is from Picasso's Blue Period.

- *The Child's Bath* by Mary Cassatt. This is the artist's most famous work.

- *Haystacks* by Claude Monet. The Art Institute is famous for these collections of Claude Monet's works. His models rose 20 feet tall outside his farmhouse, and he painted them over and over. They helped launch his career. You won't want to miss his *Water Lilies* either.

## DID YOU KNOW?

The four identical pairs of bronze sea horses that border Buckingham Fountain (301 E. Columbus Dr.; 312-742-7529; chicagoparkdistrict.com) symbolize the four states that border Lake Michigan. The sculpture in Grant Park honors Clarence Buckingham, who was a great supporter of the Art Institute. Kids like to splash in the fountain when it's hot.

- *A Sunday on La Grande Jatte* by Georges Seurat. If you get close enough, you can see the tiny dots that make up the image. It took him two years to finish the painting!

- *America Windows* by Marc Chagall. The huge stained glass was created to celebrate America's bicentennial.

- *Nighthawks* by Edward Hopper. This is Hopper's most famous painting, and it features four people in a diner.

- *The Bedroom* by Vincent van Gogh. You can also see van Gogh's self-portrait.

- *Sky Above Clouds IV* by Georgia O'Keeffe is huge. It's supposed to be of clouds from an airplane, but some people think it looks like something else.

What was your favorite?

# Are You an Impressionist?

Impressionist artists liked to paint outdoors and portray natural subjects like fields and oceans. They often worked outside.

Their style of art started in France in the mid-1800s and was called Impressionism because the artists weren't interested in painting a realistic portrayal. They wanted to create an idea or an impression instead with bright colors.

Some of the most famous impressionist artists were Edouard Manet, Camille Pissarro, Edgar Degas, Alfred Sisley, Claude Monet, and Pierre-Auguste Renoir.

They liked to portray people doing what they did every day—in a field, for example, or Degas's ballerinas—and often used their families as subjects. But they were as interested in the entire scene—everything around the person.

You can see more Impressionist paintings at the Art Institute of Chicago than anywhere outside of France. Download an app that will help guide you through the collection.

Look at the way they used brushstrokes (very thick!) and how they were able to capture the way light changed. Monet was famous for painting pictures of the same thing in different seasons, for example. There is an entire room dedicated to Monet at the Art Institute.

You could try your hand at art most weekends at the Artist's Studio for kids. It's free!

# Free Art

There's a lot of art to see in Chicago outside of museums. In fact, some is right on the street or in public parks. There's even a program to make sure that new or renovated municipal buildings and public spaces include original artwork:

- The Pablo Picasso sculpture in Daley Plaza in the Loop (50 W. Washington St.) is unnamed, but it has become one of Chicago's most famous sculptures. It's 50 feet high! You can slide down its base.

- Joan Miró's *The Sun, the Moon and One Star*, now known as *Miró's Chicago* (69 W. Washington St.), is 40 feet tall and across the street from the Picasso.

- Jean Dubuffet's *Monument with Standing Beast* (100 W. Randolph St.) is one everyone calls "Snoopy in a Blender." Kids like to crawl around inside it.

- Alexander Calder's *Flamingo* sculpture in Federal Plaza in the Loop (Dearborn and Adams Streets) is bright red. Its curved lines contrast with the steel and glass buildings.

## DID YOU KNOW?

There are free concerts all summer in Grant Park (205 E. Randolph St.; 312-742-7638; grantparkmusicfestival.com) and Millennium Park (201 E. Randolph St.; 312-742-2963; cityofchicago.org).

- Anish Kapoor's *The Cloud Gate* sculpture in Millennium Park cost $23 million. Everyone calls it "The Bean" because it looks like a bean! See how it reflects the sky and the buildings.

- Claes Oldenburg's sculpture *Batcolumn* (600 W. Madison St.) was inspired by Chicago skyscrapers, chimney stacks, and construction cranes.

- Marc Chagall's mosaic *The Four Seasons* shows six scenes of Chicago (Dearborn and Monroe Streets). It's made of thousands of chips in over 250 colors.

- There are rotating exhibits of Chicago-themed photographs at The City Gallery in the Historic Water Tower (806 N. Michigan Ave.; 312-742-0808; cityofchicago.org).

- Contemporary visual art by local artists is shown in the Chicago Cultural Center where you will also see a bronze cow outside at 78 E. Washington St. Check out the eyes— you'll see reflections of the Picasso sculpture and the Historic Water Tower (78 E. Washington St.; 312-744-6630; cityofchicago.org).

You can find a detailed list of public art at cityofchicago.org/publicart.

# Art Tells Stories

Whether you are looking at modern art and historic photographs or exploring Chicago history and culture, Chicago museum exhibits tell stories of people and their cultures. Here is a sampling of what Chicago museums have to offer kids and their parents:

> **A VISITING KID SAYS:**
> "I love the Bean. It's so cool. You can see yourself in a weird shape. The reflection isn't straight, but more curved."
> —Ellie, 14, Stillwater, MN

- **Chicago History Museum** (1601 N. Clark St.; 312-642-4600; chicagohs.org) allows you to ride a high-wheel bike down a wood-paved street, hear about the Great Chicago Fire, or dress up like a Chicago-style hot dog.

- **DuSable Museum of African American History** (740 E. 56th Place; 773-947-0600; dusablemuseum.org) is the oldest museum dedicated to African-American history, culture, and art. Admission is free on Sunday!

- **Museum of Contemporary Art** (220 E. Chicago Ave.; 312-280-2660; mcachicago.org) is one of the world's largest contemporary art museums.

- **Museum of Contemporary Photography** (600 S. Michigan Ave.; 312-663-5554; mocp.org) Is the place to see photographs of the 20th century and today.

- **National Museum of Mexican Art** (1852 W. 19th St.; 312-738-1503; nationalmuseumofmexicanart.org) showcases Mexican, Latino, and Chicano arts and culture and is a good place to explore the history of Mexico.

- **Spertus** (610 S. Michigan Ave.; 312-322-1700; spertus.edu) is Chicago's Jewish education and cultural center and has exhibits to help everyone understand the Jewish experience.

- **Swedish American Museum and The Brunk Children's Museum of Immigration** (5211 N. Clark St.; 773-728-8111; swedishamericanmuseum.org) has a hands-on exhibit that tells the story of the many Swedish children who moved to Chicago. Check out the immigrant steamship!

## TELL THE ADULTS:

If you live in Chicago and have a Chicago Public Library Card, you can check out a Kids Museum Passport at any Chicago public library for a week, which gives you entrance to 15 of Chicago's museums (chipublib.org).

The Art Institute of Chicago is always free for kids under 14. There are art-making activities, family self-guided tours, and more to make learning about art fun (artic.edu/visit/visiting-your-family). Before you visit, decide where you want to focus your attention. You can:

- Start at the Ryan Education Center where you can get gallery games and information. (The Vitale Family Room has more than 1,000 children's books, if you need a break!)

- Purchase a special Lions Trail Family Tour audio guide with 32 stops.

### DID YOU KNOW?

You can take a pedestrian bridge right from the sculpture garden of the Art Institute to Millennium Park high above Monroe Street. It is 625 feet long and a great way to check out the skyline and the lake. It's called the Nichols Bridgeway.

- Visit the drop-in Artist's Studio that features activities based on the museum's collections and exhibits.

- Take a Family Gallery Walk on a half-hour inter-active tour.

- Sign on for a special Family Workshop.

- Try the Little Studio, which offers hands-on activities for children ages 3–5 with an adult.

- On special Family Days, there are gallery games, performances, storytelling, and artist demonstrations and the chance to meet Artie the Lion, the Art Institute's mascot.

# 6
# Lions, Gorillas, Polar Bears & the Beach

# The hardest part of visiting the

**Lincoln Park Zoo** (2001 N. Clark St.; 312-742-2000; lpzoo
.org) is deciding where to go first.

Do you want to see the gorillas and the chimps? Check
out the gorilla youngsters! They learn from each other
just like you and your family do. Hear something weird?
The **Regenstein Center for African Apes** is designed to
make you feel as if you are in Africa, and that includes the
sounds. It's also home to
some of the world's
rarest creatures—
black rhinos,
pygmy hip-
pos, and dwarf
crocodiles.

A LOCAL KID SAYS:
"I went to the zoo at the holidays to
see the lights. The whole zoo was decorated.
We couldn't even see all of it."
—Robin, 13

Maybe you want to visit the polar bears, watch the sea lions play, wait for the lions to roar, or take a walk on the **Nature Boardwalk.** It has won a lot of awards for its sustainable design. It's hard to believe that this area was once a dilapidated pool! Did you see the rare black-crowned night heron nesting? Everyone can bird-watch here!

Look for the turtles basking on the boulders. The painted turtles were implanted with transponders so the biologists can monitor their health; some even have small radio transmitters. See all the fish? The pond at Nature Boardwalk has been stocked with native fish including bluegills (the state fish of Illinois), largemouth bass, and others.

Of course you don't want to miss the **Children's Zoo.** This is the place to see animals that live closer to home— black bears and river otters, red wolves and beavers. This is also the place to see what life would be like on a Midwestern farm. Have you ever seen a cow being milked?

You won't be able to pass up the **McCormick Bird House** where you can watch birds of prey fly. Did you know they are considered nature's cleanup crew? Check out the Bali mynah while you're there. It's one of the world's

A LOCAL KID SAYS:
"Walk, ride, or blade—all my favorite things to do are along the lakefront."
—Hannah, 12

rarest birds, but today, the Lincoln Park Zoo is growing the population.

Everyone loves the flamingos. Did you know they like the cold and choose to be outdoors almost all the time?

Kids say they like the Lincoln Park Zoo because it's not too big. The best part about it—besides the animals and that it's free—is that it's right in **Lincoln Park** (2045 N. Lincoln Park West; 312-742-7726; chicagoparkdistrict.com) where you can bike, in-line skate, go on a paddleboat, check out the beach, or have a picnic.

### DID YOU KNOW?

There are fewer than 25,000 polar bears left in the wild. The polar bears are among the most popular creatures at the Lincoln Park Zoo.

{ **What's Cool?** The 3-D animals, thousands of twinkling lights, and music show at ZooLights at the Lincoln Park Zoo during the holidays.

There are plenty of playgrounds too. **Adams Playground** (1919 N. Seminary Ave.; 312-742-7787; chicagoparkdistrict .com) even has a water play area in summer, and **Jonquil Playlot Park** (1001 W. Wrightwood Ave.; 312-742-7816; chicagoparkdistrict.com) has a playground that's accessible for all kids, even those in wheelchairs.

Stop in at the **Lincoln Park Conservatory** (2391 N. Stockton Dr.; 312-742-7736; chicagoparkdistrict.com). It has got 3 acres of all kinds of exotic and tropical plants and flowers. It's an especially fun place to get out of the cold in the winter. Outside, look for the migrating birds. Many stop at the Alfred Caldwell Lily Pool.

If it's summer, you're probably ready to hit the **beach.** Chicago kids don't think it's weird at all to go to a beach on a lake rather than the ocean. They think it's just as much fun. Do you?

# Who Says History is Boring?

Not at the **Chicago History Museum** near Lincoln Park (1601 N. Clark St.; 312-642-4600; chicagohs.org) it's not.

Go to the Sensing Chicago gallery and you can discover history through your nose with a Smell Map, hear the Great Chicago Fire, or dress up as a Chicago-style hot dog. Create a postcard of your favorite Chicago sight and e-mail it to a friend.

Look for the gallery stations where you might be able to test a bridge you've built or trace the path of the Great Chicago Fire. Check out the hands-on model of the John Hancock Center and learn more about the history of skyscrapers in Chicago.

You can even see how Chicago has been the Crossroads of America. Check out Chicago's first L car that was built in 1892 and travel back in time to that era. Think you would have liked to be a kid here then?

## DID YOU KNOW?

The statue *Standing Lincoln* by sculptor Augustus Saint-Gaudens in Lincoln Park was based on casts made of Lincoln's face and hands when he was alive. You can see it in the garden east of the Chicago History Museum.

# Nature in the City

Like butterflies? Get up close to 75 different species—more than 1,000 of them—at the **Peggy Notebaert Nature Museum** (2430 N. Cannon Dr.; 773-755-5100; naturemuseum .org) in Lincoln Park. The Judy Istock Butterfly Haven has colorful birds, too, all living in a big greenhouse filled with water pools, flowers, and tropical trees. There are some you'd never see outside in the Midwest. They're such pretty hues! Come at 2 p.m. and you might see new butterflies released.

The Butterfly Haven and Nature Museum are part of the Chicago Academy of Sciences, one of America's oldest scientific institutions. While you're at the museum, you can see how many different environments are found right in Chicago as you walk through a prairie, savanna, and dune areas. Listen for the sounds!

## DID YOU KNOW?

The Lincoln Park Zoo is home to 1,100 mammals, birds, reptiles, amphibians, and thousands more fish and insects. You can visit them every day of the year—for free!

Engineer your own waterway at the RiverWorks exhibit. You can reverse the flow of your river, build a dam, or turn the river into a lake.

Watch as the museum scientists and volunteers care for the animals at the museum's Living Collection. Check out Nature's Lunch Box and see how food and nature are connected. Take a walk on one of the nature trails outside.

You can learn how to identify birds by their sounds and look through binoculars to see the variety of birds right outside. What do you hear?

A LOCAL KID SAYS:
"The lake is so big that it feels like an ocean. And it's nice to live close by and go there in the summer with my friends!"
—Posey, 13

# Endangered Species and How You Can Help

An *endangered species* is an animal or plant that is in danger of disappearing completely from our planet. The Lincoln Park Zoo leads the way in wildlife conservation with zoo scientists working around the world. Many other species are *threatened*, which means that unless conservation efforts are started, they're likely to become endangered. Many of the 200 different species of animals at the Lincoln Park Zoo are rare and endangered. Animals and humans are part of one world with one ocean that is up to us to protect. Every day, you can do small, simple things to help the planet:

- Turn off lights when you leave a room. Turn off the television if no one is watching it.

- Create a recycling center in your home and recycle newspapers, glass, and aluminum cans.

{ **What's Cool?** Visiting Africa without leaving Chicago. You can go nose-to-nose with gorillas and chimps through huge glass windows at the Lincoln Park Zoo's Regenstein Center for African Apes.

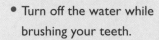

- Turn off the water while brushing your teeth.

- Use both sides of a piece of paper.

- Plant wildflowers in your garden instead of picking them from nature.

- Reduce the amount of trash you create: Reuse your lunch bag each day.

- Don't buy animals or plants taken illegally from the wild or that are not native to your area. Ask where they're from.

- Share what you know with family and friends.

A VISITING KID SAYS:
"I like the Lincoln Park Zoo because it's small and easy to get around. It's also fun to walk around the Lincoln Park neighborhood. It's near the beach, and our good friend lives there."
—Tyler, 12, New York

The Lincoln Park Zoo is one of the few free zoos in the country. There are also opportunities to give kids a sense of the Midwest while visiting:

- Experience a traditional Midwestern family farm at the Farm-in-the-Zoo, which showcases animals found on a typical Illinois farm.

- There are also two organic gardens with crops that grow in Illinois, such as corn and beans.

- The Nature Boardwalk enables you to immerse yourselves in a Midwestern prairie ecosystem—right in the heart of the city—with prairie and wetland grasses and plants, migratory birds, turtles, and even dragonflies.

A VISITING KID SAYS:
"You should definitely get postcard souvenirs of Chicago. They are everywhere."
—Jenna, 12, Antioch, IL

- The wooded habitat at the Pritzker Family Children's Zoo is devoted to North American wildlife including American black bears, red wolves, beavers, and river otters. Inside, you'll see owls, snakes, turtles, and more.

- The zoo's educational ZooTracks (lpzoo.org/education/educators-resources) is a great resource for parents as well as teachers to make a visit more meaningful.

SEE HOW MANY OF THESE ANIMALS YOU SEE AT THE LINCOLN PARK ZOO AND CHECK OFF WHAT YOU FIND!

❑ African lion ❑ Gorilla

❑ Ape ❑ Chimpanzee

❑ Polar bear ❑ Monarch butterfly

❑ Sea lion ❑ Painted turtle

❑ Bluegill ❑ Flamingo

❑ Moholi bushbaby ❑ African wild dog

❑ Red panda ❑ Green tree python

❑ Snowy owl ❑ Sichuan takin

❑ Waterbuck ❑ Bactrian camel

❑ Kenya crested guineafowl

❑ Emperor newt

DRAW PICTURES OF THE ANIMALS YOU SAW
(OR MAY SEE) AT THE ZOO!

# 7

# Deep-Dish Pizza, Flaming Cheese, Hot Dogs & Souvenirs

# Hungry? Take your pick in Chicago—

deep-dish pizza, hot dogs, burgers, or ribs.

Or maybe you'd rather have a Chinese noodle dish, pasta with meatballs, or some Indian curry. Let's not forget fish that might come straight from Lake Michigan.

You'll find all that and more in Chicago—everything from fancy restaurants that serve too many courses to count to some of the best hot dogs you've ever had. Are you okay with tomatoes on your hot dogs? That's Chicago style!

In summer, you can stop at a farmers' market and pick up yummy fixings for a picnic in the park.

Go to **Chinatown** (chicagochinatown.org) for dim sum (dumplings with all kinds of fillings) or **Greektown** (greektownchicago.org) for flaming cheese and shish kebab.

**Wentworth Avenue** in Chinatown is a good place to shop for souvenirs too—everything from candy ginger chews to teas and trinkets.

Cool off on a summer day with an **Italian ice** on Taylor Street in **Little Italy.** Visit a **tortilla factory** in **Pilsen,** Chicago's largest Mexican neighborhood.

Full yet?

A VISITING KID SAYS:
"I like eating at Ed Debevics because it is hilarious and the staff is rude on purpose."
—Matthew, 10, Florida

{ **What's Cool?** Shopping for only-in-Chicago souvenirs at Accent Chicago (John Hancock Center, 875 N. Michigan Ave.; 312-654-8125; accentchicagostore.com).

Then it must be time to do some shopping. Chicago is as fun a place to shop as eat. A lot of kids like to go to **North Michigan Avenue** where you'll find **The American Girl Place** (835 N. Michigan Ave.; americangirl.com) and the huge **Niketown** (669 N. Michigan Ave.; 312-642-6363; store.nike.com) as well as all kinds of other stores. There are a lot of famous Chicago sports pictures in Niketown as well as every kind of Chicago sports gear you might want, especially for basketball.

Got your American Girl doll with you? Make a reservation to bring her to tea or lunch at The American Girl Place. They've got special chairs and dishes for the dolls!

A VISITING KID SAYS:
"I like shopping on the Magnificent Mile. Some of my favorite places are Forever 21, the Disney Store, and the Hershey's store, or actually all the candy places."
—Caitlyn, 17, Charlestown, IN

{ **What's Cool?** NIKEiD studio at Niketown where you can personalize and customize your Nike gear. You might see a pro athlete browsing new sneakers next to you.

Check out the vertical shopping malls. They go up, like a tall building, so they don't take up as much room on a city block. Stop in **Macy's** (111 N. State St.; 312-781-4483; visitmacyschicago.com) and get a **Frango chocolate bar.** Chicago kids have been eating Frango chocolates since before your grandparents were born. They're yummy!

See the **Water Tower** on Michigan Avenue (835 N. Michigan Ave.; 312-440-3166; shopwatertower.com)? The tower was originally built to house a large pump drawing water from Lake Michigan. It was one of the few buildings to survive the Great Chicago Fire and so it became a symbol of old Chicago. Today there are shops here.

> **DID YOU KNOW?**
>
> People call the stretch of North Michigan Avenue from the Chicago River to Oak Street the Magnificent Mile (themagnificentmile.com). There are more than 450 shops!

While you are in the neighborhood, you may also want to go to the top of the **John Hancock Center** (875 N. Michigan Ave., Ste. 2605.; 888-875-VIEW; jhochicago.com/en). It's not the tallest building in Chicago, but a lot of kids think its observatory has the best panoramic views of the lake and skyline.

If you like browsing in little stores, you'll probably want to hit some other Chicago neighborhoods, like Lincoln Park's **Armitage Avenue.**

Like the Cubs? You'll find everything **Cubbies** on Clark Street (between Diversey Avenue and Addison Street) near Wrigley Field.

Look for souvenirs that will remind you of your visit. What's your pick?

A LOCAL KID SAYS:
"Chicago pizza is the best pizza in the world: deep-dish with the most cheese you have ever seen on a single pizza and sauce on top. You bite in and it tastes perfect."
—Samantha, 13

# Pizza Like None Other

Ready to dig in? Chicago-style deep-dish pizza was invented at Pizzeria Uno in Chicago in 1943. Some say Uno's founder, Ike Sewell, a former University of Texas football star, came up with the idea. Others believe that Uno's pizza chef Rudy Malnati developed the recipe.

Today, everyone who comes to Chicago wants to try it. The crust is very thick, and deep-dish pizza is baked in a round, steel pan more like a cake pan than a pizza stone. The dough is pressed up onto the sides of the pan, forming a bowl for a very thick layer of toppings.

Be prepared to wait! The thick layer of toppings used in deep-dish pizza requires a longer baking time. The toppings are assembled opposite from what you would expect, with the cheese going on the crust first, followed by meat and vegetables. The top layer is tomato sauce.

You can get Chicago pizza at **Giordano's** (giordanos.com), **Lou Malnati's** (loumalnatis.com), **Pizzeria Uno** (unos.com), and **Gino's East** (ginoseast.com), among other places. You can get Chicago pizza elsewhere, but it won't taste exactly the same. Some people love it so much they have it shipped from Chicago to them.

You can still get thin-crust pizza in Chicago but expect it to be cut in squares rather than triangles.

**What do you like on top of your pizza?**

# Souvenir Smarts

Baseball cap, Windy City sweatshirt, or mini Willis Tower? Maybe you want to bring home a tin of Chicago's famous Garrett Popcorn to share with your friends. The hardest part will be deciding what to buy.

- Shop smart! That means talking to your parents about exactly how much you may spend. Save your pennies and quarters before you visit. Some families save loose change in a jar to use for vacation souvenirs. Got any birthday money you can add?

- Do you want to use your money for one big souvenir or several smaller ones?

- Resist those impulse buys and think about choosing something you could only get in Chicago.

- Start a collection! Buy stickers to put on your reusable water bottle. Collect pins or patches to put on your backpack.

**What else could you collect?**

A LOCAL KID SAYS:
"It is very fun to go to the Taste of Chicago in the summer and try food from lots of different cultures."
—Michael, 9

# Eating Smart on Vacation

Vacations are a good time to try different foods than just what is on a kids' menu. That's especially true in Chicago where you'll find restaurants that feature food from all around the world as well as vegetables, fruits, and meats from local farmers. Here's how you can eat healthier and try new foods:

- Split a portion of something with your brother or sister, your mom or dad.

- If there is something you like on the grown-up menu, ask if you can get a half portion or order an appetizer size.

- Opt for fruit as a snack instead of chips or candy.

- Visit a local farmers' market and talk to the farmers.

- Drink water rather than a soda.

## DID YOU KNOW?

There are nearly two dozen farmers' markets in Chicago neighborhoods. You can find fresh fruits, vegetables, and flowers. Talk to the farmers who grew them! There's even a farmers' market in the Loop—Chicago's Downtown Farmstand (66 E. Randolph St.; chicago farmersmarkets.us).

# Souvenirs Worth Taking Home

Here are some places where you'll find souvenirs you can't find anywhere but in Chicago:

- **Bye Bye Chicago** prides itself on selling everything Chicago—team baseballs and shirts, coffee cups, magnets, and postcards. (224 S. Michigan Ave.; 312-235-0471; byebyechicago.com)

- **Accent Chicago** is at the base of the John Hancock Center and has everything you would want with Chicago on it! (835 N. Michigan Ave.; 312-944-1354; accentchicagostore.com)

- **Chicago Architecture Foundation Store** is the place for books about Chicago architecture and all things Frank Lloyd Wright, the famous architect. You'll love the model kits for famous Chicago buildings. (224 S. Michigan Ave.; 312-222-3080; architecture.org)

A LOCAL KID SAYS:
"It's cold in Chicago, but if you wear a jacket, hat, and gloves, being outside is totally worth it!"
—David, 14

- *Chicago Tribune* **Store** is on the lower level of the Tribune Tower. You can buy a copy of the cover of the newspaper from the day you were born! (435 N. Michigan Ave.; chicago tribunestore.com)

- **Hancock Observatory Shop** is the place to get prints or specialty items with your picture so you can remember the view from way up high, along with many other fun items to help you remember your trip. (875 N. Michigan Ave.; 888-875-8439; jhchicago.com)

- **Lillstreet Gallery** has many handcrafted pieces made by local and national artists. Although this is a little farther out of the way off the Brown Line Montrose stop, you can also check out the gallery and the classes going on. (4401 N. Ravenswood at Montrose; 773-769-4226; lillstreetgallery .com)

# Some Great Chicago Eateries for Kids & Families

- **Ed Debevics** (640 N. Wells St.; 312-664-1707) is the quintessential short-order diner, serving burgers, shakes, and other standards in a classic setting with a 1950s-themed decor. What makes the place truly memorable, though, is the comically rude service. Their motto, after all, is "If you like what you're eatin', order more. If you don't—there's the door."

- **Eleven City Diner** (1112 S. Wabash Ave.; 312-212-1112; elevencitydiner.com), conveniently located by the Museum Campus, serves up generous plates of delicatessen favorites like pastrami, brisket, and Reuben sandwiches.

- **Francesca's Little Italy** (1400 W. Taylor St.; 312-829-2828; miafrancesca.com) on Taylor Street is in the heart of Chicago's historic Italian neighborhood and offers a wonderful

## DID YOU KNOW?

The Taste of Chicago (mostly known as The Taste) is the world's largest food festival, held every year in July in Chicago in Grant Park. There's music, rides, and every kind of food you can think of. (cityofchicago.org)

There are more than 5,000 restaurants in Chicago.

array of pastas, pizzas, and other favorites. Kids are sure to love the scoop of gelato at the end of every meal, too!

- **Hot Doug's** (3324 N. California Ave.; 773-279-9550; hotdougs.com), the so-called "Sausage Superstore and Encased Meat Emporium," is well regarded as one of the best places to feast on Chicago-style hot dogs, Polish sausages, bratwurst, and other favorites. For the more adventurous, try some of the ever-changing special sausages like an Apple and Cinnamon Pork Sausage with Cherry-Roasted Garlic Chutney and White Cheddar Cheese Curds!

- **Lou Mitchell's** (565 W. Jackson Blvd.; 312-939-3111; loumitchellsrestaurant.com) is at the beginning of historic Route 66 in downtown Chicago. They're famous for their breakfast, but the best thing about a visit to "Uncle Lou's" may be the box of Milk Duds that kids get right when they walk in the door!

- **Smoque BBQ** (3800 N. Pulaski Rd.; 773-545-7427; smoquebbq.com) is the place to be if you're in the mood for great barbecue. Try their famous Texas-style beef brisket or their St. Louis–style ribs, and don't forget the mac n' cheese!

Kids don't want to be limited to kids' menus. Nor do you want them eating a steady diet of chicken fingers and fries on vacation. Of course, you want to treat yourselves on vacation and sample food a city is famous for—like Chicago pizza. But we all want to eat healthier on vacation, too. First Lady Michelle Obama has made combating childhood obesity and eating healthy a top priority with her **Let's Move! Campaign** (letsmove.gov). Here's how she suggests you eat healthier on vacation:

- Planning ahead and packing nutritious snacks whenever possible is a good way to avoid resorting to less healthy options.

- Choose restaurants that give us healthier options and call on other businesses to make similar changes.

- Visit a farmers' market with the kids.

- Get the kids thinking about vacation as an adventure for their taste buds as much as a chance to explore new places.

# HELP THE HOT DOG FIND ITS WAY TO CHICAGO!

# 8
# Music & Theater

# Trumpet, violin, or guitar?

Whatever you play, you'll find Chicago musicians making terrific music in grand concert halls, in parks in the summer, on street corners, and in small clubs across the city. There are outdoor music festivals all summer.

Chicago is especially famous for the **blues and jazz** that have inspired generations of country and rock 'n' roll performers. This type of music arrived with Southerners who

A VISITING KID SAYS:
"Millennium Park is cool for concerts in the summer. The sound bounces back so you can hear and it has a cool vibe. There are usually lots of people who come out for the shows."
—Tori, 16, Miles City, MT

**DID YOU KNOW?**

The first *Home Alone* movie was filmed in a northern Chicago suburb.

settled here looking for a better life in the early years of the 20th century. Ever since, Chicago has been known for this music, starting on the South Side where blues musicians still perform every night as well as elsewhere in the city. Can you imagine that when one musician named Muddy Waters decided to electrify his guitar for a new sound, it was so revolutionary that it changed music for years to come?

Chicago is just as famous for theater, too—especially **comedy.** A lot of famous actors got their start here. Can you name one?

Do you like dance? There is a lot of dance here. In fact, **Ballet Chicago** (balletchicago.org) is where young dancers come to train, and as part of that, they perform around Chicago.

{ **What's Cool?** Going with your family to an outdoor concert under the stars in Chicago in the summer.

The **Civic Orchestra of Chicago** is made up of young performers, and they share music across the city, too. Tickets to their concerts at Symphony Center (220 S. Michigan Ave.; 312-294-3420; cso.org) are free!

Like folk music and guitars? The **Old Town School of Folk Music** (oldtownschool.org) has special concerts for kids and monthly open microphone sessions for teens to perform.

There are plenty of special performances just for kids whether you want to see the Chicago Symphony Orchestra, find out what an opera is like, or attend a play that was written just for kids.

You've got your choice of children's theater companies in Chicago:

- **Chicago Children's Theatre** (chicagochildrenstheatre.org). Ask about Red Kite Adventures—multisensory theatrical experiences for children.

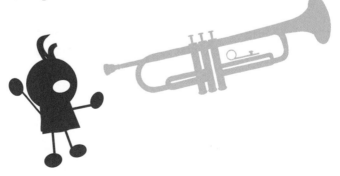

- **Emerald City Theatre Company** (emeraldcity theatre.com), which you can see perform at the Apollo Theater Center in Lincoln Park and at Broadway Playhouse at Water Tower Place.

- The famous **Steppenwolf Theatre** (1650 N. Halsted St.; 312-335-1650; steppenwolf.org) produces two shows each year for kids.

Did you know that the **Chicago Symphony Orchestra** has been playing in Orchestra Hall for more than 100 years? That's because the acoustics are so terrific. You'll hear it if you attend a concert here. You might rather

{ **What's Cool?** Hearing a professional orchestra play something you played with your school orchestra.

spread out on a blanket on the grass and hear the orchestra play in Millennium Park in the summer.

Many Chicago families make it a tradition to go to a concert in the summer or a play at the holidays—like **A Christmas Carol at the Goodman Theatre** (goodman theatre.org).

Maybe you can make seeing a performance part of your vacation tradition. What's your pick?

A LOCAL KID SAYS:
"Going to the concerts in the summer outside is way better than going to see a concert other places because you can run around and play games."
—Janice, 11

**What's Cool?** Seeing a Broadway musical—in Chicago. Touring companies perform in Chicago all the time. Look for schedules and tickets on broadwayinchicago.com.

# Musical Instruments

Bassoons, cymbals, and tambourines—they're all part of an orchestra just like violins and cellos, flutes and oboes, trumpets and French horns. An orchestra is a large group of musicians playing instruments from four different groups—strings, woodwinds, brass, and percussion.

The strings section includes violins, violas, cellos, and basses. Woodwinds could be flutes, piccolos, oboes, English horns, clarinets, bass clarinets, bassoons, and contrabassoons. If you were playing in the brass section, you might have a trumpet, French horn, trombone, or tuba. Percussion includes snare drums, bass drums, cymbals, gongs, and other instruments, like xylophones and bells.

**Do you play an instrument?**

# Great Desserts

- **The Cupcake Counter** (229 W. Madison St.; 312-422-0800; thecupcakecounter.com) has made-from-scratch cupcakes in flavors like carrot, pumpkin, and cookies and cream. Besides tasting delicious, these cupcakes make you feel good because The Cupcake Counter donates a portion of its proceeds to charitable organizations in the community.

- **Hoosier Mama Pie Company** (1618 W. Chicago Ave.; 312-243-4846; hoosiermamapie.com) has more than 10 fresh baked sweet pies to choose from each day. They also have quiches and savory pies, so you can make a lunch out of it! Check the Twitter page to find out what flavors of pie are in the oven today.

- **Mario's Italian Lemonade** (1068 W. Taylor St.; 312-829-0672) in Little Italy is a great place to cool down during a hot Chicago summer. Try some of the delicious frozen

lemonades made with real fruit, but be careful not to get a brain freeze!

- **Scooters Frozen Custard** (1658 W. Belmont Ave.; 773-244-6415; scootersfrozencustard.com) is one of the best places in the city to try frozen custard, a type of ice cream that is amazingly creamy and delicious. Try one of their "concretes," a blend of frozen custards and toppings that is so thick you can eat it upside down!

- **Vosges Haut-Chocolat** (520 N. Michigan Ave.; 312-644-9450; vosgeschocolate.com) is a Chicago-based chocolate company that is probably best known for its milk chocolate bacon bars, but it offers a wide array of other chocolates with exotic ingredients. Check out the Michigan Avenue boutique while you're in town.

## DID YOU KNOW?

The Rolling Stones named themselves after the Muddy Waters 1950 song, "Rollin' Stone." Waters' blues influenced generations of musicians who followed him. A strip of 43rd Street is called Muddy Waters Drive. His real name was not Muddy Waters, of course. His grandmother nicknamed him Muddy when he was a young boy because he liked to play in a muddy creek.

## TELL THE ADULTS:

Chicago is a great place to share music and theater with the kids—and it doesn't have to be expensive:

- During the summer, free concerts are held in Millennium Park on Wednesday, Friday, and Saturday evenings. (205 E Randolph St.; 312-742-7638; grantparkmusicfestival.com)

- In the summertime, the Chicago Symphony Orchestra plays at Ravinia in Highland Park on the North Shore. It's a great bet to take a picnic and sit on the grass! You can take the train. (200 Ravinia Park Rd., Highland Park; 847-266-5100; ravinia.org)

A LOCAL KID SAYS:
"Every summer we see a play at the Chicago Shakespeare Theater at Navy Pier. Then we have a picnic by the lake."
—Anna, 7

- Apollo Chorus of Chicago, founded in 1872, sings at churches around town. (apollochorus.org)

- The Chicago Symphony Orchestra (cso.org) has a special family matinee series and other special family concerts.

- The Lyric Opera of Chicago (lyricopera.org) offers special family productions during the year and student matinees.

- The Chicago Shakespeare Theater (800 E. Grand Ave.; 312-595-5600; chicagoshakes.com) on Navy Pier has a family series with shorter Shakespeare productions as well as fairy tales, interactive concerts, and musical theater.

- Lookingglass Theatre Company was cofounded by actor David Schwimmer and uses lots of acrobatics. Children's tickets to Sunday matinees are just $25 with the purchase of an adult ticket. (821 N. Michigan Ave.; 312-337-0665; lookingglass theatre.org)

- At the Joffrey Ballet of Chicago (joffrey.com) before certain performances, you can meet dancers, choreographers, and other members of the creative team at the "Meet the Artists" program.

9
Play Ball!

# Cubs or Sox?

That's a very important question in Chicago.

Chicagoans take their sports very seriously and that's certainly the case during baseball season when the city cheers on two major league teams.

Typically those living on the South Side and in the south suburbs root for the **White Sox;** those on the North Side and in the northern suburbs support the **Cubs.**

You've probably never met fans like Cubs fans. They take pride in their team despite the fact that they haven't

A LOCAL KID SAYS:
"I've been a Cubs fan since I was 7. I know that they'll win a World Series soon!"
—Elizabeth, 14

won a World Series in more than a century! Those who grow up in Chicago rooting for the Cubs tend to stay fans no matter where they move.

Even if you don't go to a game, you'll get a sense of how much people on the North Side love their Cubbies if you are anywhere near Wrigley Field on a game day. Old-fashioned Wrigley Field is so much in the middle of the neighborhood— called Wrigleyville—that some fans can even watch from the rooftops of their apartments.

Which Chicago baseball team do you like? Make sure to remember your mitt if you go to a game. If you're really lucky, you might catch a foul ball!

When it comes to football, soccer, basketball, or soccer, Chicagoans have it a lot easier and all unite behind one team. And they don't lose faith if their teams lose—as they often do. That just makes them root for them all the more!

As soon as the weather warms up, Chicagoans **get outside** and, especially if you're visiting in spring, summer, or fall, you can join them:

- **Running, biking, or in-line skating** along the lakefront. Find out where the bike paths are with chicago bikes.org maps; you can rent bikes and in-line skates from bikechicago.com.

- Playing **tennis** on Chicago's public courts. Try the ones in Grant Park.

- **Swimming** in Lake Michigan at one of Chicago's 33 beaches (chicagoparkdistrict.com).

- **Kayaking.** Take a spooky Ghosts and Gangsters tour on the Chicago River or watch the Navy Pier fireworks from the water (wateriders.com).

**DID YOU KNOW?**
Chicago is one of just a few cities that has two major league baseball teams—the White Sox on the South Side and the Cubs on the North Side.

{ **What's Cool?** Chowing down on a famous Chicago hot dog at a baseball game.

- **Fishing.** In April, Chicagoans come out to try to catch smelt, tiny fish that come into the harbors to spawn. You'll find maps online from The Illinois Division of Fisheries (ifish illinois.org).

A LOCAL KID SAYS:
"The White Sox are better because they have a better field, team, and mascot. Their food is better, too."
—Donte, 9

And even though it's really cold in Chicago in the winter, Chicago kids don't let that keep them inside. If you're visiting in winter, you can:

- **Ice-skate** at Daley Bicentennial Plaza and at the McCormick-Tribune Ice Rink operated by the Chicago Park District (chicagoparkdistrict.com).

- **Sled.** The park district runs a big sledding hill near Soldier Field (chicagoparkdistrict.com).

Whatever you want to try when you visit, you'll find local kids outside having fun.
Ready?

# Shoeless Joe Jackson

Say it ain't so, Joe!

After the White Sox lost the 1919 World Series to the Cincinnati Reds, Joe Jackson and seven other White Sox players were accused of accepting $5,000 each to throw the Series.

There was a grand jury investigation, and legend has it that as Jackson was leaving the courthouse during the trial, a young boy begged of him, "Say it ain't so, Joe." Even though Jackson's exchange with the young fan might not have happened that way, the story remains an oft-repeated part of baseball history.

In 1921 a Chicago jury acquitted Jackson and his seven teammates of wrongdoing. Nevertheless, the commissioner of baseball said that all eight accused players were ineligible for any future MLB play.

Jackson—he was nicknamed "Shoeless," from early in his career after playing a minor league game in his socks because

## DID YOU KNOW?

There are more than 550 parks in Chicago, and you can often find a pickup basketball game in progress.

he'd gotten blisters from new spikes—never played in organized baseball after the 1920 season and maintained his innocence until he died.

The famous baseball movie *Field of Dreams* tells the story of an Iowa farmer played by Kevin Costner, who hears a voice telling him to build a baseball field on his farm so Shoeless Joe Jackson could play ball again.

Still today, people believe Jackson, a great and record-setting player, was innocent, but because he remains on MLB's ineligible list, he can't be elected to the National Baseball Hall of Fame. You can find out more about Jackson on the website shoeless joejackson.com.

**What do you think?**

A LOCAL KID SAYS:
"I love going to see the Wolves! Hockey is my favorite sport, and the games are not too crowded so you can sit near the action."
—David, 14

# Know Your Chicago Sports Legends

**Michael Jordan** ended his Chicago Bulls career with the highest per-game score average in NBA history.

**Bobby Hull,** the Blackhawks player, is considered an all-time great hockey player.

**Mike Ditka** is the only person to have won a Super Bowl as a player (for the Dallas Cowboys), assistant coach (Cowboys), and head coach (Chicago Bears).

**Ozzie Guillen,** the former beloved player for the White Sox and former White Sox coach, is loved for making the White Sox world champions in 2005—bringing a World Series trophy to Chicago for the first time in nearly a century.

**Ernie Banks** was the first player to have his number retired by the Cubs.

**Gale Sayers, Walter Payton,** and **Dick Butkus** are all legendary players from the 20th-century Chicago Bears.

## DID YOU KNOW?

Michael Jordan and the Chicago Bulls won six of the eight basketball championships from 1991–98 against five different teams from the NBA Western Conference. The Bulls' misses were in 1994 and 1995 when Jordan missed most of two seasons while playing baseball.

# Learning History at a Baseball Game

Going to Wrigley Field isn't like going to most other ballparks. There's a lot of history here! Wrigley Field is baseball's second oldest park. The only park older is Fenway Park, home of the Boston Red Sox.

- The first National League game at the ballpark was played April 20, 1916. A bear cub was in attendance! In 1920, after the Wrigley family (yes, the chewing gum family) bought the team, the park became known as Cubs Park. It was named Wrigley Field in 1926 in honor of William Wrigley Jr., the Cubs' owner.

- In case you are wondering, Ernie Banks' uniform No. 14 and Ron Santo's No. 10 are imprinted on flags that fly from the right field foul pole. Billy Williams' No. 26 and Ryne Sandberg's No. 23 fly from the left field foul pole.

- Are you sitting on the bleachers? The Wrigley Field bleachers and scoreboard were constructed in 1937, and the original scoreboard remains intact. See how the score-by-innings and the pitchers' numbers are changed by hand?

- See the famous ivy vines? They were first planted more than 75 years ago and balls do get lost there—and hit into the stands! Got your mitt handy?

## TELL THE ADULTS:

Whatever season you visit Chicago, there will be professional sports going on and some of the most enthusiastic fans you'll find anywhere:

- **NFL Chicago Bears,** Soldier Field (1410 S. Museum Campus Dr.; chicagobears.com). Dress warm!

- **NBA Chicago Bulls** and **NHL Chicago Blackhawks,** United Center (1901 W. Madison St.; bulls.com and chicagoblackhawks.com)

- **MLB's Chicago Cubs,** Wrigley Field (1060 W. Addison St.; 773-404-2827; cubs.com).

- The **Chicago Fire** soccer team, Toyota Park (7000 S. Harlem Ave., Bridgeview; 708-594-7200; chicago-fire.com) and **Chicago Sky WNBA,** Allstate Arena (6920 Mannheim Rd., Rosemont; 847-635-6601; chicagosky.net)

- **MLB's Chicago White Sox** at US Cellular Field (333 W. 35th St.; 312-674-1000; whitesox.com)

- Women's soccer's **Chicago Red Stars** at Benedictine University Sports Complex (5700 College Rd., Lisle; 772-697-8699; chicagoredstars.com)

## SPORTS WORD SCRAMBLE

Can you unscramble these Chicago-area sports teams and then write it what sport each team plays!

**Team Name**                               **Sport**

SEARB _____  _____

ACKBLAWKSH _____  _____

LUBLS _____  _____

BCUS _____  _____

ERIF _____  _____

EDR TARSS _____  _____

ITEWH SXO _____  _____

KYS _____  _____

See page 155 for the answer key.

A VISITING KID SAYS:
"I bought a Blackhawks shirt for a souvenir. I really enjoy watching them play."
—Emma, 15, Stillwater, MN

# 10

# Beyond Chicago:
## Sand Dunes, Waterslides & Bears

# Climb up or slide down?

You can climb up a tall sand dune at the famous **Indiana Dunes National Lakeshore** (nps.gov/indu) or take your pick of waterslides at the **Wisconsin Dells** (wisconsindells .com). Both are an easy drive from Chicago and favorites with Chicago kids.

The Indiana Dunes have a lot more than those famous dunes, though. There are beaches on Lake Michigan that stretch for miles where you can try kite flying, build a giant sand fortress, or play Frisbee or beach volleyball.

Like to watch birds? Just beyond the beach, there are 45 miles of trails that are home to hundreds of species.

Maybe you'd rather explore the shoreline. How many different colored rocks can you find?

### DID YOU KNOW?

The first dunes of Indiana were formed approximately 15,000 years ago by the last of the Ice Age glaciers.

You can become a Junior Ranger when you visit. Download the activity guide from the website or pick one up at the visitor center. Take part in a ranger program while you're there, and make sure to stay on the trails!

As you walk around, consider that this wonderful place almost became a big industrial complex, but was preserved through the efforts of dedicated environmentalists who convinced Congress to turn it into a national park.

This place is big! The park is comprised of over 15,000 acres of dunes, oak savannas, swamps, bogs, marshes, prairies, rivers, and forests. It contains 15 miles of Lake Michigan shoreline in Indiana from Gary to Michigan City.

Did you know the big sand dunes actually move? Mount Baldy

**What's Cool?** Hiking up Mount Baldy, the tallest moving sand dune at the Indiana Dunes National Lakeshore. It's 126 feet high!

moves about 4 feet a
year—whenever the
northwest wind exceeds
7 mph. Crazy!

Leave the sand
behind for a different
kind of experience play-
ing in and around the water. Welcome
to the Wisconsin Dells—the water park capital
of the world. Did you know the idea of indoor water
playgrounds started here?

That's smart thinking for a region with such a
long winter! No wonder local kids like to go to the Dells
in winter with more than 20 indoor water parks to choose
from, many with hotels attached. There are more than 200

A LOCAL KID SAYS:
"All the water parks at the
Wisconsin Dells are really fun, and
it's not too far way from Chicago."
—Quincy, 14

waterslides and one of the world's largest surf pools (with 9-foot waves) at **Mt. Olympus Water & Theme Parks** (1881 Wisconsin Dells Pkwy.; Wisconsin Dells, WI 53965; 800-800-4997; mtolympuspark.com).

Take your pick of plunge slides, tube rides, racing speed slides, bowl drops, water roller coasters, and lazy rivers. There's also go-karts and minigolf, horseback riding, and a free outdoor skate park called **SK8 Park.**

There's plenty of outdoor water park fun in the summer, too, especially at **Noah's Ark Water Park** (1410 Wisconsin Dells Pkwy., Wisconsin Dells, WI 53965; 608-254-6351; noahsarkwaterpark.com), the largest in the country. It's got "Quadzilla," a 4-lane mat racing ride, 51 watersides, two huge wave pools, two lazy rivers, and for younger kids, four kiddie water play areas.

Got your swim goggles?

## DID YOU KNOW?

Just touching a blue poison frog is enough to get a dose of poison that could be deadly.

# Talking to the Animals

See the dolphins jump! Go eye to eye with a giant grizzly bear. Dress up like a bird.

You can do all that and more at the **Brookfield Zoo** (3300 Golf Rd., Brookfield, IL 60513; 708-688-8000; brookfieldzoo.org) outside Chicago in Brookfield, Illinois. You can even see what the animals do at night at a special zoo sleepover. At the Hamill Family Play Zoo, touch animals, lend a hand to building habitats, examine an animal x-ray, and help plant a garden. Just in this area are 300 animals!

The largest exhibit ever undertaken at Brookfield Zoo is Great Bear Wilderness featuring North

A VISITING KID SAYS:
"The Brookfield Zoo was much bigger than other zoos I've been to."
—Vincenzo, 14, Austin, TX

American animals: grizzly bears, polar bears, bison, eagles, and Mexican gray wolves. See the bald eagle? You can watch the wolves interact without them knowing you're there. Watch the polar bears and grizzlies swim from the underwater viewing area.

Ready to go to Africa? You'll feel like you're there at the Habitat Africa! exhibit that takes you to the rain forest in one area and the savanna in another. See the herd of giraffes? Watch the African painted dogs that play just like you do.

There is so much to see at this zoo—leopards and lions and tigers in the Big Cat exhibit, rare birds and reptiles (have you ever seen a bright blue poison frog?), naked mole rats and other desert creatures, and animals that call the rain forests of Asia home like the clouded leopards. Look in the trees, on the ground, and in the shadows to find different species. Check out the crocodiles in The Swamp! Did you notice that there are different species in the same area, just like in the wild?

The Brookfield Zoo is famous for its efforts—since the zoo was founded—to conserve and protect the animals. What can you do to help?

# Prairie Style

Frank Lloyd Wright was only 22 when he designed the **Frank Lloyd Wright Home and Studio** in Oak Park (951 Chicago Ave., Oak Park, IL 60302; 312-994-4000; gowright.org).

Oak Park is just 10 miles west of Chicago. If you are interested in architecture, you can see several Frank Lloyd Wright homes where people still live—from the outside anyway—on Chicago Avenue and Forest Avenue in Oak Park. He built over two dozen houses here—in less than 15 years—and also lived here for a time with his wife and six kids.

Check out the Unity Temple he designed—it's a National Historic Landmark—and likely a lot different than other houses of worship you've visited.

## DID YOU KNOW?

Frank Lloyd Wright was the most famous American architect of the 20th century (gowright.org). He designed more than 1,000 projects, including several in Chicago and nearby Oak Park where he lived and worked.

The great American novelist Ernest Hemingway started writing as a reporter for his high school newspaper in Oak Park, Illinois, where he grew up.

You'll know Prairie Style when you see it—Frank Lloyd Wright was the master. The roofs are low-pitched, and the houses usually are made of brick and stone with small windows. The idea is the house is part of the natural world. Do you think you'd like to live in one?

The house Ernest Hemingway grew up in here couldn't be more different. His boyhood home is just a few blocks from the Frank Lloyd Wright Home and Studio. There's a **Hemingway Museum** there (200 N. Oak Park Ave., Oak Park, IL 60302; 708-524-5383; ehfop.org).

You can see what it was like to have lived here at the beginning of the 20th century if you visit Ernest Hemingway's birthplace.

When Frank Lloyd Wright and Ernest Hemingway were boys, no one knew they'd grow up to be world-famous or that their influence would continue long after they were gone. Each was a trailblazer—Hemingway in his style of writing and Wright in his architectural designs.

Do you think any of your friends could grow up to accomplish something no one has done before? How about you?

# TELL THE ADULTS:

There is a lot to see beyond Chicago that parents and kids will love:

**Evanston:** Ten miles north of Chicago is the home of Northwestern University and a great place to visit right along the lake. Learn about Native American tribes in the Midwest and elsewhere at the **Mitchell Museum of the American Indian** (3001 Central St., Evanston, Illinois 60201; 847-475-1030; mitchellmuseum.org) with more than 10,000 Native American artifacts. Kids will like shopping in downtown Evanston along with the college kids.

**Skokie:** Twelve miles north of Chicago is home to the **Illinois Holocaust Museum and Education Center** that also opens the dialog about speaking out against genocide (9603 Woods Dr.; Skokie, IL 60077; 847-967-4800; ilholocaustmuseum.org).

**Wilmette:** Fourteen miles north of downtown Chicago is home to the **Baha'i Temple House of Worship** (100 Linden Ave.; Wilmette, IL 60091; 847-853-2300; bahaitemple.org), the US center of the Baha'i faith, and the visitor's center has exhibits that explain it. The huge temple has nine sides and is spectacular when the dome is lit up at night.

**Wheaton:** Thirty miles west of Chicago you'll find **Cantigny Park** (1S151 Winfield Rd., Wheaton, IL 60189; 630-668-5161; cantigny.org)—a 500-acre estate with a military history museum, gardens, a public golf course with a separate course for kids, and a mansion that houses the **Robert R. McCormick Museum.** He was the former owner of the *Chicago Tribune.*

**Springfield:** The state capital city about 200 miles southwest of Chicago is where you can celebrate President Lincoln, including visiting the only home he ever owned (426 S. 7th St., Springfield, IL 62701; 217-391-3221; visit-springfieldillinois.com) and the **Presidential Library and Museum** (212 N. 6th St., Springfield, IL 62701; 800-610-2094; visit-springfieldillinois.com).

**New Buffalo, Michigan:** This is the place in the Midwest to go for surfing and paddleboarding.

**Milwaukee, Wisconsin:** Less than 2 hours north of Chicago, Milwaukee (visitmilwaukee.org) is home to:

- **The Harley Davidson Museum** (400 W. Canal St., Milwaukee, WI 53201; 1-877-HD-MUSEUM; harley-davidson.com) with hundreds of bikes.

- The lakefront **Milwaukee Art Museum** (700 N. Art Museum Dr., Milwaukee, WI 53202; 414-224-3200; mam.org).

- Miller Park where you can watch the **MLB Brewers** play (1 Brewers Way, Milwaukee, WI 53214).

- The huge **Summerfest music festival** (summerfest.com).

**Madison, Wisconsin:** About 3 hours northwest of Chicago, Madison (visitmadison.com) boasts the largest capitol building outside Washington and the Dane County Farmers' Market, one of the country's biggest, that's famous for its **Wisconsin cheeses.** Rent a bike and take a ride—there are 120 miles of trails—or go kayaking. The **Madison Museum of Contemporary Art** boasts a rooftop sculpture garden (227 State St., Madison, WI 53703; 608-257-0158; mmoca.org). while the **University of Wisconsin** has a huge arboretum and campus to explore if you want to show kids what a big university campus looks like.

# Water Park Smarts

Here's what the Wisconsin Dells, the water park capital of the world, says you need to make the most of your day slipping and sliding and playing in gigantic water playgrounds:

- Dry clothes for the ride home.

- Sunscreen, applied generously and often. Remember that the indoor water parks have big outdoor areas in the summer.

- Swim socks are a good bet because you can keep them on during the rides. You can also stow your flip-flops in shelves at the base of most rides.

- Sunglasses with strap. Sun reflecting off water makes sunglasses a necessity, and you don't want to lose them on a waterslide!

- Quarters. You'll need them for the storage lockers for all your other essentials.

- Don't forget your towel!

What a Trip!

I came to Chicago with:

_____

_____

_____

The weather was:

_____

_____

_____

We went to:

_____

_____

_____

We ate:

_____

_____

_____

We bought:

_____

_____

_____

I saw these famous Chicago sites:

_____

_____

_____

My favorite thing about Chicago was:

_____

_____

_____

My best memory of Chicago was:

_____

_____

_____

My favorite souvenir is:

_____

_____

_____

You had such a great time in Chicago! Draw some pictures or paste in some photos of your trip!

# Index

## A

*A Christmas Carol* at the
  Goodman Theatre, 110
Abbott Hall of Conservation, 43
Abbott Oceanarium, 47
Accent Chicago, 91, 98
Adams Playground, 78
Addams, Jane, 25
Adler Planetarium, 35, 42, 45, 55
Alfred Caldwell Lily Pool, 78
Allstate Arena, 126
American Girl Place, The, 92
Andersonville, 19, 26
Apollo Chorus of Chicago, 114
aquatic show, 47
Aqua Tower, 20
architects, famous, 4, 25, 98, 136
Armitage Avenue, 94
art, 6, 34, 58, 59, 61, 62, 65, 66,
  68, 99, 140
Artie the Lion, 71
Art Institute of Chicago, 58, 59,
  62, 65, 70
Artist's Studio, 65, 71

## B

Baha'i Temple House of
  Worship, 138
Ballet Chicago, 107
Banks, Ernie, 124, 125
baseball, 118, 120, 122, 124, 125,
  126, 140
basketball, 122, 124, 126
beaches, 75, 77, 78, 85, 120, 130
Bean, The, 58, 59, 60, 67, 68
Bike and Roll Chicago, 35

biking, 35, 77, 120, 140
Black History Month, 22
blues, 106
Bluhm Family Terrace, 62
Broadway musicals, 110
Brookfield, Illinois, 134
Brookfield Zoo, 134, 135
Brunk Children's Museum of
  Immigration, The, 69
Buckingham Fountain, 60, 63
bugs, 43
Build-A-Bear, 31
Burnham, Daniel, 25
Butkus, Dick, 124
butterflies, 80
Bye Bye Chicago, 98

## C

Calder, Alexander, 66
Candy Sugar Shoppe, 31
Cantigny Park, 139
Capone, Al, 25
Caribbean Reef, 47
carousels, 31
Cassatt, Mary, 63
Chagall, Marc, 64, 67
cheese from Wisconsin, 140
Chicago Academy of
  Sciences, 80
Chicago Antique Market, 21
Chicago Architecture Foundation
  Store, 98
Chicago Bears, 119, 124, 126
Chicago Blackhawks, 124,
  126, 127
Chicago Bulls, 25, 124, 126

Chicago Children's Museum, 32, 34, 36, 37
Chicago Children's Theatre, 108
Chicago CityPASS, 11
Chicago Cubs, 18, 94, 118, 120, 124, 126
Chicago Cultural Center, 7, 67
Chicago Fire, 126
Chicago Fire Academy, 3
Chicago Greeter, 11
Chicago History Museum, 68, 79
Chicago River, 2, 4, 5, 16, 120
Chicago's Downtown Farmstand, 97
Chicago Shakespeare Theater, 114, 115
Chicago Sky, 126
Chicago Symphony Orchestra, 108, 109, 114
*Chicago Tribune,* 22, 139
*Chicago Tribune* Store, 99
Chicagoween, 23
Chicago White Sox, 118, 120, 121, 122, 124, 126
Children's Zoo, 76
Chinatown, 26, 91
Chinese New Year, 22
Christmas Around the World, 49
Cinco de Mayo, 22
City Gallery, The, 67
Civic Orchestra of Chicago, 108
Clark Family Lab, 55
Cloud Gate. *See* Bean, The
collecting, 34, 96
comedy, 107
Crater Maker, 45
Crown Fountain, 59
Crown PlayLab, 55

Crystal Gardens, 32
Cupcake Counter, The, 112

D
deep-dish pizza, 90, 94, 95
Degas, Edgar, 65
desserts, 112
Devon Avenue, 26
dinosaurs, 42, 52
Disney, Walt, 49, 59
Ditka, Mike, 124
Dubuffet, Jean, 6, 66
DuSable Museum of African American History, 68

E
Ed Debevics, 91, 100
Eleven City Diner, 100
Emerald City Theatre Company, 109
endangered animals, 77, 82, 135
environment, protecting the, 9, 43, 50, 82, 131
Evanston, Illinois, 138

F
Fab Lab, 48
Fairy Castle dollhouse, 49
Family Fun Tent, 60
Family Gallery Walk, 71
Family Workshop, 71
Farm-in-the-Zoo, 84
Ferris, George W., 33
Ferris wheels, 4, 8, 30, 31, 32, 33
Field Museum, 35, 42, 43, 44, 55
Field of Dreams, 123
firefighting, 3, 36
Fire Prevention Week, 10
fireworks, 23, 31, 120
firsts introduced in Chicago, 8

fishing, 121
foods, ethnic, 19, 26, 91
football, 124, 126
fountains, 32, 58, 59, 60, 63
Francesca's Little Italy, 100
Frango chocolate bar, 93
Frank Lloyd Wright Home and
   Studio, 136
free activities, 11, 18, 58, 60, 65,
   66, 68, 70, 77, 80, 114

**G**

Gang, Jeanne, 20
Garrett Popcorn, 31
Gemini 12, 45
gemstones, 44
Gino's East, 95
Giordano's, 95
go-karts, 133
Gold Coast, the, 17
Graceland Cemetery, 19
Grant Park, 35, 63, 66, 100, 120
Great Bear Wilderness, 134
Great Chicago Fire, 2, 10, 20, 32,
   68, 79, 93
Greek Independence Day, 22
Greektown, 22, 26, 91
Guillen, Ozzie, 124

**H**

Habitat Africa!, 135
Hamill Family Play Zoo, 134
Hancock Observatory Shop, 99
Hands-on Science, 55
Harley Davidson Museum,
   The, 140
Haunted Village, 23
Hemingway, Ernest, 136, 137
Hemingway Museum, 137
Hendrickson, Sue, 52

Highland Park, 114
Historic Water Tower, 67
hockey, 123, 124, 126
Holidays of Light, 49
Home Alone movie, 107
Hoosier Mama Pie Company, 112
Hopper, Edward, 64
horseback riding, 133
hot dogs, 79, 90, 99, 101, 120
Hot Doug's, 101
Hull, Bobby, 124
Hull House, 25
Hyde Park, 20
Hyde Park Hair Salon, 20

**I**

ice-skating, 6, 23, 58, 121
Illinois Holocaust Museum and
   Education Center, 138
Impressionists, 62, 65
Independence Day, 23, 31
Indiana Dunes National
   Lakeshore, 130, 131
instruments, 111

**J**

Jackson, Shoeless Joe, 122
jazz, 106, 108
Joffrey Ballet of Chicago, 115
John Hancock Center, 17, 79,
   94, 98
John Hancock Observatory, 6
Jonquil Playlot Park, 78
Jordan, Michael, 25, 124
Judy Istock Butterfly Haven, 80
Junior Ranger, 131

**K**

Kapoor, Anish, 67
kayaking, 120, 140

Kids Museum Passport, 70

L

lakefront, 5, 76, 120
Lake Michigan, 19, 30, 31, 34, 63, 93, 120, 130, 131
Lakeview, 18
Let's Move! Campaign, 102
Lillstreet Gallery, 99
Lincoln, Abraham, 79, 139
Lincoln Park, 18, 35, 77, 79, 80, 85, 109
Lincoln Park Conservatory, 78
Lincoln Park Zoo, 74, 77, 80, 82, 83, 84, 85
Lions Trail Family Tour, 70
Little Italy, 26, 91, 112
Little Saigon, 19
Little Studio, 71
Lookingglass Theatre Company, 115
Loop, The, 5, 6, 11, 17, 97
Lou Malnati's, 95
Lou Mitchell's, 101
L, The, 6, 21, 79
Lurie Garden, 60, 69
Lyric Opera of Chicago, 115

M

Macy's, 93
Madison Museum of Contemporary Art, 140
Madison, Wisconsin, 140
Magnificent Mile, 92, 93
Magnificent Mile Lights Festival, 23
Manet, Edouard, 65
Mario's Italian Lemonade, 112
maze, 32

McCormick Bird House, 76
McCormick, Robert R., 22, 139
Michael's Museum, 34
Millennium Park, 35, 58, 59, 60, 66, 67, 69, 70, 71, 106, 110, 114
Miller Park, 140
Milwaukee Art Museum, 140
Milwaukee Brewers, 140
Milwaukee, Wisconsin, 139
minigolf, 133
Miró, Joan, 66
Mitchell Museum of the American Indian, 138
model railroad, 44
Monet, Claude, 63, 65
Mount Baldy, 131
Mt. Olympus Water & Theme Parks, 133
Museum Campus, 35, 42
Museum of Contemporary Art, 68
Museum of Contemporary Photography, 69
Museum of Modern Art Chicago, 67
Museum of Science and Industry, 4, 44, 48, 49, 54, 55
music, 58, 60, 66, 77, 100, 105, 140

N

National Museum of Mexican Art, 69
Nature Boardwalk, 75, 84, 85
Navy Pier, 17, 23, 30, 31, 32, 33, 34, 114, 115, 120
Near North, 17
neighborhoods, 16, 19, 26

New Buffalo, Michigan, 139
Nichols Bridgeway, 70
NIKEiD, 92
Niketown, 92
Noah's Ark Water Park, 133
North Avenue Beach, 18, 75
North Michigan Avenue, 92, 93
North Side, 120
Northwestern University, 138

O

Oak Park, Illinois, 136
Obamas, The, 7, 20, 25, 102
Oh Yes Chicago!, 31
O'Keeffe, Georgia, 64
Oldenburg, Claes, 67
Old Town, 18
Old Town School of Folk
    Music, 108
outer space, 45

P

paddleboarding, 139
parades, 2, 22
Payton, Walter, 124
Pegboard Challenge in the
    Tinkering Lab, 34
Peggy Notebaert Nature
    Museum, 80
Picasso, Pablo, 7, 63, 66
Pilsen, 20, 26, 91
Pissarro, Camille, 65
Pizzeria Uno, 95
playgrounds, 78, 85
Polar Play Zone, 47, 55
Potawatomi Indians, 17
Prairie Style, 136
Pritzker Family Children's
    Zoo, 85

Pritzker Pavilion, 60

R
Ravinia, 114
Red Kite Adventures, 108
Regenstein Center for African
    Apes, 74, 82
Renoir, Pierre-Auguste, 65
Richard J. Daley Center, 7
Riverwalk, 16
Robert R. McCormick
    Museum, 139
Route 66, 101
Ryan Education Center, 61, 70

S
safety, 10, 24, 36
Saint-Gaudens, Augustus, 79
Sandberg, Ryne, 125
sand dunes, 130, 131
Santo, Ron, 125
Sayers, Gale, 124
scary ride advice, 37
Scooters Frozen Custard, 113
Seurat, Georges, 64
Shedd Aquarium, 35, 42, 46, 47,
    50, 51, 55
shopping, 91, 92, 93
Sisley, Alfred, 65
SK8 Park, 133
skating, 77, 120, 133
Skating in the Sky, 6
Skokie, Illinois, 138
Skydeck, 13
skyline, 3, 21, 59, 94
skyscrapers, 3, 8, 25, 34, 79
sledding, 121
Smoque BBQ, 101
soccer, 126

Soldier Field, 126
South Loop, 17
South Side, 107, 120
souvenirs, 18, 23, 31, 49, 84, 91,
    94, 96, 98, 127
Spertus, 69
sports, 117
sports legends, 124
Springfield, Illinois, 139
Staley the Bear, 119
Steppenwolf Theatre, 109
St. Patrick's Day, 2, 22
Sue the *T. rex,* 43, 52
Sullivan, Louis, 25
Summerfest, 140
surfing, 139
Swamp, the, 135
Swedish American Museum, 69
Swedish Bakery, 19
swimming, 120

T

Taste of Chicago, 23, 96, 100
tennis, 120
Thanksgiving Day, 23
theater, 108
Thorne Miniature Rooms, 62
Time Out Chicago Kids, 10
Tinkering Lab, 34
tombstone that looks like a
    baseball (William Hulbert's
    grave), 19
Touch Gallery, 62
tourism website, 10
Toyota Park, 126
Transporter FX, 31
Tribune Tower, 22, 99

U

Ukrainian Village, 20
underground walkways, 19
University of Chicago, 20
University of Wisconsin, 140
Uptown, 19, 26
US Cellular Field, 126

V

van Gogh, Vincent, 64
Vosges Haut-Chocolat, 113

W

water parks, 132, 141
waterslides, 130, 133
Waters, Muddy, 107, 113
Water Tower, 3, 93
Water Tower Place, 109
Wentworth Avenue, 91
Wheaton, Illinois, 139
Williams, Billy, 125
Willis Tower, 5, 6, 8, 13
Wilmette, Illinois, 138
Winfrey, Oprah, 25
Winter WonderFest, 23
Wisconsin Dells, 130, 132, 141
Wolves, The, 123
Wood, Grant, 62
World's Columbian Exposition,
    4, 33
Wright, Frank Lloyd, 98, 136
Wrigley Field, 18, 94, 119,
    125, 126
Wrigleyville, 18, 119

Z

ZooLights, 77
ZooTracks, 85

# Answer Keys

## Chicago Word Search (p. 12)

| W | R | I | G | L | E | Y | F | I | E | L | D | F |
|---|---|---|---|---|---|---|---|---|---|---|---|---|
| I | U | A | B | V | B | R | P | N | T | B | Z | E |
| N | M | B | M | R | I | O | A | R | H | P | A | R |
| D | T | R | R | B | G | E | B | I | E | B | R | R |
| Y | P | E | C | I | S | A | C | M | L | Y | A | I |
| C | I | T | Y | T | H | A | T | W | O | R | K | S |
| I | I | S | Q | L | O | R | I | V | O | H | O | W |
| T | D | E | Z | A | U | N | O | M | P | E | B | H |
| Y | N | G | Y | I | L | C | J | A | R | G | A | E |
| S | E | C | O | N | D | C | I | T | Y | I | M | E |
| Y | F | E | G | E | E | H | L | R | E | M | A | L |
| J | U | R | H | D | R | H | A | N | C | O | C | K |
| E | C | N | A | S | S | R | S | E | W | R | O | N |
| I | B | E | T | J | L | W | Q | O | P | D | B | C |
| N | M | W | I | L | L | I | S | T | O | W | E | R |

## Secret Word Puzzle (p. 38)

Navy Pier Ferris Wheel

154

**Sports Word Scramble (p. 127)**

BEARS (Football)

BLACKHAWKS (Hockey)

BULLS (Basketball)

CUBS (Baseball)

FIRE (Men's Soccer)

RED STARS (Women's Soccer)

WHITE SOX (Baseball)

SKY (Women's Basketball)

# About the Author

Award-winning author Eileen Ogintz is a leading national family travel expert whose syndicated Taking the Kids is the most widely distributed column in the country on family travel. She has also created TakingtheKids.com, which helps families make the most of their vacations together. Ogintz is the author of seven family travel books and is often quoted in major publications such as *USA Today*, the *Wall Street Journal*, and the *New York Times*, as well as parenting and women's magazines on family travel. She has appeared on such television programs as *The Today Show*, *Good Morning America*, and *The Oprah Winfrey Show*, as well as dozens of local radio and television news programs. She has traveled around the world with her three children and others in the family, talking to traveling families wherever she goes. She is also the author of *The Kid's Guide to New York City*, *The Kid's Guide to Orlando*, *The Kid's Guide to Washington, DC*, and *The Kid's Guide to Los Angeles County* (Globe Pequot Press).